SEX & THE SINGLE PERSON

SEX & THE SINGLE PERSON

Dealing Honestly with the Need for Intimacy

Robert G. DeMoss, Jr.

Zondervan Publishing House
Grand Rapids, Michigan

A Division of HarperCollinsPublishers

Sex and the Single Person
Copyright © 1995 by Robert G. DeMoss, Jr.

Requests for information should be addressed to:

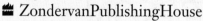 ZondervanPublishingHouse
Grand Rapids, Michigan 49530

Library of Congress Cataloging-in-Publication Data

DeMoss, Robert G.
    Sex and the single person : dealing honestly with the need for intimacy
 / Robert G. DeMoss, Jr.
      p. cm.
    ISBN 0-310-20009-1 (pbk. : alk. paper)
     1. Single people—Religious life. 2. Single people—Sexual behavior.
 3. Single people—Conduct of life. 4. Sex—Religious aspects—Christianity.
 5. Intimacy (Psychology)—Religious aspects—Christianity. 6. Chastity.
 I. Title.
 BV4596.S5D46 1995
 248.8'4—dc20   95-558
                                                  CIP

Names have been changed to protect the privacy of the individuals involved.

Published in association with the literary agency of Alive Communications, Inc., 7680 Goddard Street, Suite 200, Colorado Springs, Colorado 80920.

Interior design by Joe Vriend

Printed in the United States of America

---

01 02 03 04 05 06 /❖ DC/ 20 19 18 17 16 15 14 13 12 11 10

To my angel,
Let

Contents

Acknowledgments

If I were to tell you that I know of a bridge built out of eggs, you'd think I was overdue for a trip to the funny farm. But such a marvel of nature exists! Located behind Lima's presidential palace is the Roman-style Puente de Piedra, or "Bridge of Stone." When it was built back in 1610, local engineers mixed hundreds of thousands of egg whites into the mortar—they thought it would strengthen the bridge.

Evidently, they were right. Nearly four centuries of earthquakes have rocked the city of Lima—including one in 1746 that basically flattened the city. But the Puente de Piedra has survived intact.[1]

Some things seem so hard to believe.

For me, the thought of writing this book would have been as impossible to imagine as a bridge made with eggs if it were not for the help of so many. At the outset, I'd like to offer several words of appreciation.

In the fall of 1992, I was invited to participate as a panel member for a Focus on the Family broadcast entitled, "Singles: Dealing with Sexuality." The questions Dr. James Dobson asked of us over this three-day series prompted further private reflection about my singleness and the issue of sexuality. Thank you Dr. Dobson for stimulating my thinking on such an intensely personal subject. The roots of this book grew out of those musings.

To all of the singles who took the time to fill out my survey, thank you for sharing from your heart. Many of you have wanted to know how I would have answered that eleven-page questionnaire. You're holding my response!

I'd like to offer a special word of appreciation to Charles and Lee Hennessee-Gradanté. Your West Palm Beach condo was the perfect place to pen these pages. I won't soon forget the priceless sunrises, the gentle breezes, and the endless view of the Atlantic Ocean that served as a constant source of inspiration for my writing.

Likewise, Bob McDonald, I'm thankful for those late-night chats at Murray's, not to mention use of your "anointed chair."

Writing a book is usually not possible without the support of a research assistant. I had the best any author could ask for in Leticia Bermudez. In addition to the thorough research, your stenography skills captured my spoken ideas in our brainstorming sessions. Not only did you pitch a tent inside the local library, you worked overtime interacting with every page of the manuscript.

Now that the book is finished, would it be too much to ask you for a date?

I owe a word of thanks for additional research provided at the last minute by Glenn Stanton and Craig Osten.

It was an unusual move, Michael Geer. But I thank you nonetheless for advertising for a wife on my behalf—without my knowledge. Did you get that idea from *Sleepless in Seattle*? (Who says the media doesn't influence behavior!) And, Jim and Kim Thomas, thank you for offering to sing a wedding song at such time as the Lord sends the right woman along.

I must send a warm bear hug to Jon and Marylois Gibson for taking such a personal interest in advancing my quest for a godly wife. The boat ride was unforgettable! And I value your advice regarding my ideas for this book.

Greg—"I'll see if we can move the deadline just one more time"—Johnson and Rickly—let's make a deal—Christian, thanks for believing in me and this project. You guys are the best!

My deepest appreciation goes to my incredibly supportive family. Becky and Jack, thanks for organizing the prayer team and for locating all of those comics. Steve and

Sharon, you'll find your stream of faxed insights reflected in these pages—they were invaluable. John and Alison, thanks for organizing your six little angels to pray for their Uncle Bob. Timothy, thanks for lending a hand locating and transcribing the Becker tune.

Mom and Dad, I know that if there was a way to wrap you both up in a big red bow and pass you around to other singles the world would be a much better place. Thank you for your spiritual guidance, constant prayers, and generous loving touch that have surrounded me all the days of my life—especially during the writing of this book.

And Dad, your editorial input, daily calls and faxes, the steady stream of articles, and the giant-sized poster of encouragement were beyond the call of duty. I love you and Mom so much!

Most of all, thank you, Jesus, for your example. You lived your earthly life—single. You fulfilled your calling and died—single. You rose again as a single. Yet you never complained or compromised your commitment along the way. Thank you for setting the mark.

Introduction

If two lie down together they keep warm,
but how can one be warm alone?

—*Ecclesiastes 4:11* NAS

Lord, give me chastity—but not yet.

—*Saint Augustine[1]*

I have a theory: Singleness is a product of the fall of mankind. Think about it. Everybody who lived *before* the Fall was married!

Granted, my hypothesis is a bit of a theological stretch. Yet for many of us singles, that's exactly the way we feel. Being unattached in a world made for couples presents some real challenges—especially when it comes to dealing with our sexuality.

For me—a thirty-seven-year-old virgin—I desire to one day give my mind, soul, and *body* to a spouse. I long for intimacy, and yearn to experience the pleasure of God's gift of sex. There are times when every cell in my body cries out for a loving touch. Yet I may go days—if not weeks—without a hug or warm embrace.

At the same time, the intimacy I crave is nothing like the trash that television models. Take, for example, the sex-charged ad campaign by Dejaiz—a national clothing outlet. In one sequence, a handsome guy applies the sexual advance on *seven* different girls—one for each day of the week. In similar fashion, Merry-Go-Round showed what appeared to be an unmarried couple intimately engaged. As he removed her shirt, she aggressively yanked his belt out. The slogan? "Clothes that are as fun to take off as they are to put on."

Casual sex, multiple partners? No thanks!

How about you?

Do you feel like the average high school student knows more about sex than you do, primarily because you've elected to play by God's rules? Has the carpet in your apartment become threadbare from your nightly pacing—waiting for the phone to ring? Do you think God has withheld something good from you for no apparent reason? Are you tempted to compromise your standards in order to "find out" what the rest of the world seems to already know?

I completely empathize with you.

Or perhaps you're single again. Your spouse may have died, but your *body* certainly didn't. Maybe your partner walked away from your marriage, but your hormones are very much at home. In both instances, death or divorce brought an end to the intimacy you once shared. Now what?

These situations are complicated in a number of ways. For starters, we live in an over-sexed society, one where sexual purity is passé—even among a number of Christian singles. Josh McDowell, author of the "Why Wait?" campaign, noted, "Contrary to what I had assumed, Christian young people were as sexually active as their unsaved friends."[2]

And, if you're like me, you've yet to find a practical book on the subject of single sexuality written by an *unmarried* author—someone who is actually living it! This book corrects that inequity.

A similar condition often exists in ministries to singles. My friends and I used to privately snicker when our singles pastor (who, I might add, was *married*) would talk with us about abstinence. "Right! You can engage in sex anytime, and you're going to talk to us about chastity?"

Understandably, you might think reading—or, in my case writing—a book on the subject of single sexuality will be about as much fun as having your fingernails pulled out. So why should you join me for the following discussion?

Simple. In the pages that follow, we'll discover that marriage and sex should *not* be our objective—rather, becoming a godly lover is the goal. Along the way, we'll explore sexuality for singles and acquire appropriate ways to express and enjoy intimacy this side of marriage. And, thanks to dozens of singles who have responded to a special survey, we'll eavesdrop on the experiences of others who share our feelings and learn from their insights.

A unique feature of this book is a chapter tackling the tricky situation that dating in the nineties presents. To borrow an advertising slogan from Dodge trucks, "The Rules Have Changed." With the reality of AIDS, the way we singles select a potential mate has been permanently changed—for the worse, I'm afraid. Properly equipped, there's no reason for us to withdraw from the human race!

On a personal level, I've made an invaluable discovery. I've learned that as a single adult, I regularly experience an emotional cycle—one that has dire consequences if I fail to address it properly. Identifying and understanding the way this cycle can potentially wreak havoc on my sexuality has enabled me to say no to sex for thirty-seven years, and say yes to becoming that awesome lover God would have me be. I'm confident you'll find that discussion most helpful.

> **Marriage and sex should not be our objective—rather, becoming a godly lover is the goal.**

So, put down the personals page . . . cancel the computerized companion service . . . hang up the 900-HOT-DATE line. Instead, pour yourself a cup of coffee. Find a quiet spot where you and I can lean on each other's shoulder to share a few private moments. I have a hunch our examination of this rather personal subject may surprise—and encourage—you! I look forward to what God—the Author of sex and all human intimacy—would have us discover together.

PART ONE

If God Loves Me, Why Am I Still Single?

CHAPTER 1

Virgin Territory

I always thought of losing my virginity
as a career move.
—*Madonna*[1]

It's possible to wait. Not everybody is doing it.
—*A.C. Green, Los Angeles Lakers*[2]

I love sex!

Quite frankly, there are days when it feels as if every fiber in my body longs for it. In fact, during those periods, I question if I can contain the God-given hormones inside of me. The tug-of-war rages. I know in my heart God calls me to wait. Yet the hormones lighting a fire in my libido put even the strongest commitment to chastity to the test. Thankfully, by his grace, I'm still a virgin at thirty-seven—even if at times I feel like the *last* American virgin.

Many skeptical and degrading comments have been hurled at me over the years because of my sexual standards. "How did you possibly remain sexually inactive all of those years?" "I've *never* met a virgin male as old as you, Bob." "How'd you do it? Cold showers?" "Is there something *wrong* with you?" "Do you need to see a doctor about your condition?"

A letter from Terry is telling. She writes, "I must communicate how I felt when you informed the audience at the seminar of your chaste single status. Amazed! I was shocked and pleased you exist. Hope abounds. You see, I am a 19 thirty-three-year-old single, never married, virgin woman. I've been gulping down lost hope for a while because I thought the best I might get (pardon my being blunt) would be a widower, and at worst—a divorced man with seven kids and an unhappy ex-wife." She concludes, "Good and godly men, especially single and over thirty, are hard to find. You're a treasure."

Although nobody has had the nerve to ask me, I'm sure some have secretly wondered, "Bob, are you really gay?" These comments sting. And yet, I don't blame people for wondering about my sanity or secret sexual orientation. According to virtually every report on sexual behavior I've read, statistically speaking, by my age only one-half of one percent of men are still virgins. This is due to premarital sexual choices as well as marriage.

First Sexual Experience by Unmarried Teen Boys

By age 15:	33%
By age 16:	50%
By age 17:	66%
By age 18:	72%
By age 19:	86%

Source: Allan Guttmacher Institute, using latest available data from 1988.

Guys who choose to be chaste aren't the only individuals who are treated like freaks of nature or social outcasts. A number of women filling out my single survey for this book believe they experience *stronger* emotional turmoil than men regarding their virginal status. How so? They agree that both sexes encounter pressure to perform, as well as the associated danger of contracting a sexually transmitted disease (STD). However, they're quick to point out that women run the added risk of pregnancy.

In other words, if a female caves into the pressure and engages in sex, she has a triple set of issues at stake: her loss of virginity, STD's, and the very real matter of conception. Once, while at a delightful dinner, my date lamented this very situation. She was caught right in the middle of the "damned if I do, damned if I don't" syndrome. She put it this way, "I feel like I have a capital 'V' *branded* onto my forehead!"

Frankly, it's unimportant to determine who encounters more stress over the decision to ignore their hormonal "cry of the wild." What matters is to discover *how* we singles can properly deal with our sexuality—especially when our American culture holds the virtue of virginity and sexual restraint in low regard. Likewise, we need to come to terms with the fact that marriage and sex should *not* be our objective—rather, becoming a godly lover should be. I might underline that's been the focus of my life (for reasons that will soon become clear).

In addition, we'll learn that sexual purity is an *incredible* gift from God—in spite of what you might hear to the contrary on the radio.

Spontaneous Combustion

Speaking of radio, I've personally experienced the media's overt antagonism toward moral purity. An interview on the Los Angeles-based KFI-AM news/talk station says it all.

The date was January 14, 1994—one that I'll not soon forget. I was invited to be a guest on the "Stephanie Miller Show" to discuss trading cards. Not just your basic baseball cards. These collectibles were allegedly created to increase AIDS awareness. Oh, did I mention each pack included a condom in lieu of bubble gum?!

Evidently, I was invited to "discuss" these cards on KFI because of a statement I made on "Entertainment Tonight." I told "ET": "When we swap bubble gum for condoms, we reduce the gift of sex to that of a casual handshake. And we fail to teach teens that the *best* sex is sex within marriage." I added, "I'm not against sex. I'm against the misuse of the wonderful gift of sex."

With an opinion like that, KFI felt I'd make an interesting guest—or, should I say, target. Over the course of the show, Stephanie Miller broadcast her unbridled contempt for my position on virginity to an audience of thousands.

> **I'm not against sex. I'm against the misuse of the wonderful gift of sex.**

Incidentally, we'll pick up the interview *after* the AIDS trading cards debate. You see, in Miller's mind, the issue really wasn't AIDS awareness. It was the absurdity of the abstinence position. "I'm just saying I think it is a joke to ask for total abstinence," she objected. "I think people are still going to want to have sex." Our conversation proceeded as follows:

Bob: I might mention I'm thirty-six and I'm single and I'm a virgin, and I'm proud to say that. Not everybody is doing it. And that's why I feel personally assaulted when kids say they can't wait. My goodness, what do they think I've been doing. I mean, restraint is possible. It's not easy. But I think it's a better solution.

Stephanie: Bob? Between you and me, you're gonna blow up. Do something. Hurry. You're gonna explode I think. Are you thirty-six really?

Bob: Yes, I am.

Stephanie: Bob, for God's sake!

At this point in the discussion, the interview was concluded. After she said her forced pleasantries, I left the airwaves. However, I had requested a taped copy of the entire show. Some of Miller's most degrading statements—not to mention her complete repugnance at my virginity—were aired after she discontinued our conversation. Have a listen.

Stephanie: Did you hear what I heard? Ha, ha! What did he say? He's thirty-six? Bob needs to get laid. Someone call the station now.... I mean, seriously, he's thirty-six. He's gonna blow up. His head's gonna explode! ... Let's go to Julie in La Mirada. Welcome to KFI, Julie.

Caller: I wanted to call in support of Bob DeMoss.

Stephanie: Yes, from Focus on the Family, who's a thirty-six-year-old virgin.

Caller: Yes, but you know what? I was a twenty-four-year-old virgin when I got married.

Stephanie: Yeah. But, Julie, I ...

Caller: And I didn't blow up. We have a beautiful sex life.

Stephanie: Yeah, but you're not a guy. And ...

Caller: Well, my husband was twenty-eight—and he was a virgin when we got married.

Stephanie: But, Julie, Bob is thirty-six-years-old.... Here's my point. How representative of most men is a thirty-six-year-old virgin guy gonna be?

Caller: It's not representative—and that's the unfortunate thing.

Stephanie: When he's saying we should be teaching abstinence, how is that very representative of most men? Thirty-six ...

It's hard to miss how much this news shocked Miller. She couldn't get over the fact that I was thirty-six—and a male virgin. She'd probably faint to learn I'm now thirty-seven and remain so. What's more, I don't have an illegitimate child running around. I'm not financially consumed by child support. I don't have a single sexually transmitted disease, and I sleep at night without sexual memories and guilt haunting my mind.

Furthermore, contrary to her predictions, I have yet to experience spontaneous combustion! There's one last caller worth eavesdropping on. Her name was Lynn from Santa Barbara, California.

Caller: What I wanna know is what happens if they never meet anyone that will marry them?

Stephanie: You blow up. I mean, basically, don't you? (laughing)

Caller: (laughing, too) Uh, single for the rest of their life!

Stephanie: He's gonna hit forty and it's just gonna be [using a sound effects record, Miller inserted the sound of a massive explosion].

Caller: He must be pretty bad if he hasn't married anyone up until now—that even wants to go to bed with him or marry him.

Stephanie: Yeah. Excuse me, but I think some of these [men] just can't find anyone to make it with. I don't think it's so much control. Do you? (laughter)

Caller: (laughter) I mean, sex is a normal drive. It's not dirty.

Stephanie: I agree, I agree. Although, the more *abnormal* it is the more fun I find it.

Preparing for the Priesthood?

Stephanie Miller is not alone in her contempt for my dissenting position on the "play safe" and "safe sex" messages. For much of my life I've felt alienated by classmates, peers, or associates who have mocked my commitment to chastity. If you've made a pledge to sexual purity, or if you have the guts to do so after reading this book, you'll be able to identify with the feelings of rejection and scorn I've experienced—especially as you take a public stand.

Two angry letters from junior high readers responding to my column on music in a teen magazine come to mind and are worth reprinting. Like Stephanie Miller, they took strong exception to my stand on sexual purity. After all, I've made it a practice to publicly challenge the morally bankrupt sexual attitudes of many popular musicians.

In defense of Janet Jackson's salacious song about sex in public places ("Any Time, Any Place"), Jenny wrote, "I think if Janet Jackson wants to have sex in public with whomever she wants that's just fine. . . . There's nothing wrong with premarital sex as long as the people involved mutually agree."

Darcey stated, "Who says premarital sex is a sin? I bet you're not able to say no. In fact, I've never met a guy who could wait for sex until marriage. Isn't it a fact that most guys lose their virginity by seventeen? Wake up, Bob. Stop living in the Stone Age." Darcey added several spicy words to make her point. These two impressionable girls and more young people than we'd like to imagine have the wrong impression about remaining a virgin until marriage. It's safe to say they, much like Stephanie Miller, believe it's an impossible, even undesirable goal.

Their casual attitudes toward sex unquestionably fuel the epidemic of sexually transmitted diseases plaguing our nation. According to reports by the Centers for Disease Control in Atlanta, more than 33,000 new cases of an STD are reported *every day* in America. That's alarming!

Why, then, are teens like Jenny and Darcey so indifferent?

In part, the answer lies in the way we're programmed every day of our lives. Television, music, films, and even advertising all take a swipe at abstinence. Consider, for instance, the 1991 fall television lineup. Granted, TV programs routinely model poor sexual behavior. But this season many sitcoms *preached* the dangerous message that it's okay to engage in sex as long as you are "emotionally prepared" and "play safe."

Leading the charge was ABC's *Doogie Howser, M.D.* As

Doogie turned eighteen, he found himself possessing the distressing disease of virginity. Before millions of teenaged viewers, Doogie declared: "A man is a lot of things, but he's *not* a virgin." There you have it young men of America. According to the Hollywood elite, engaging in sex is *fundamental* to manhood.

The script writers of ABC's *Roseanne* followed Doogie's deplorable lead. About the time Doogie was doing his "manly" thing, Roseanne's teenage daughter Becky announced her premarital sexual activity. Without batting an eye, Roseanne gladly provides Becky with help to go on the pill—just to be safe. Meanwhile, across the dial, Fox's *True Colors* found eighteen-year-old Terry Freeman ridiculed for his virginity.

> According to the Hollywood elite, engaging in sex is fundamental to manhood.

Such programs share the common thread of intolerance toward people of sexual purity. Although not quite as brash as British author Charlotte Bingham, they subscribe to the same school of thought. Bingham once asserted, "An isolated outbreak of virginity . . . is a rash on the face of society. It arouses only pity from the married, and embarrassment from the single."[3]

Libido Logic

Take a minute to reread the radio transcript with Stephanie Miller, as well as the feisty letters from Darcey and Jenny. As you do, try to get to the bottom of their abhorrence to the abstinence message. I noted five underlying concerns with chastity. Frankly, it wouldn't surprise me if you have had some of these questions or were tempted to agree with some of their positions.

I'll be the first to admit that, as a virgin, I've had to wrestle with these arguments. Saying no to sex for two decades while virtually everyone I know makes excuses to "fool around" has been tough—and will continue to be so. However, if you settle these matters in your mind *before* the heat of passion drives you to the brink of compromise, you'll be in the best position to stick to your convictions.

Let's evaluate these widely held assertions and concerns one at a time.

What happens to you if you never get married and don't have sex?

According to Stephanie Miller, "You blow up." Well, perhaps the government should issue Hefty bags to all virgins. That way if they accidentally blow up while in a public place, at least the clean-up would be more readily facilitated!

If I never have sex, I'll still grow old and die of natural causes. Or maybe some other calamity will take my life. Whatever the Lord has in store for my departure, I can assure you that nobody ever "died of virginity." Personally speaking, I've found it helpful to remind myself that sex is a *drive*—not a *need*. We *need* air, food, sleep, and water to exist. The sexual expression is *optional*.

It goes without saying that sex is an incredible part of life—so wonderful is sexual intimacy, I'm determined to follow God's instruction book, which plainly says "Wait." Hear me: I'll wait *even at the risk of never having sex!* Why? If sex is worth having, it's worth having the right way. Period. End of rationalization.

When you and I resolve to start—or continue—waiting, the apostle Peter warns us that there will be many naysayers—false teachers who will urge us to disregard the truth about sexual sin. He writes in 2 Peter 2:2, "Many will follow their evil teaching that there is nothing wrong with sexual sin" (LB). Peter then reminds us (v. 10) that the Lord "is especially hard on those who follow their own evil, lustful thoughts."

Sex is a drive—not a need.

Speaking of lustful thoughts, have you ever watched the behavior of some construction workers when an attractive female strolls past their project? Does the expression "cat call" come to mind? I mention that because Jesus was a carpenter. As such, my guess is that he was well-tanned and muscular. No doubt he worked without his shirt when the Mediterranean temperatures rose to uncomfortable levels.

I'm confident that, unlike his construction colaborers, Jesus didn't gawk at the females—or respond to the overtures by those women who might have been attracted to his physique. He was able to control his very real human sexual drives. As a matter of fact, when he completed his purposes on Earth, Jesus died on a cross—an unmarried virgin.

Throughout his life, the Lord demonstrated that marriage and sex should *not* be our objective—rather, becoming a godly lover is the goal.

Virgins just can't find anyone to go to bed with them. If they could, they would.

Allegations like these couldn't be farther from the truth. I have had many opportunities to abandon my commitment to abstinence. Sexual temptations abound for virgins ... they just don't act upon such enticements. Take, for instance, pro-basketball star A.C. Green. This handsome 6'9" athlete has played with the best of them, including the L.A. Lakers and the Phoenix Suns. Yet at twenty-nine, A.C. doesn't play the field. And, I might add, his outspokenness as a virgin didn't put a damper on his chances for a dalliance.

"As a professional athlete, I have to deal with groupies in many cities," says Green. "It seems as though my teammates and I are often confronted by young women wanting to meet us from the time we arrive to the time we depart. They hang out everywhere—airports, hotel lobbies, restaurants." So much for the idea that virgins have no options. Green admits, "Not many resist their advances. I don't know how many virgins there are in the NBA, but you can probably count them on one hand." Including the steadfast Green.

His bottom line scores big points with me. Green explains, "Don't get me wrong. Sex itself isn't bad. It's just a matter of *when* to experience it. God created it for enjoyment, but he also reserved it for marriage. So I'm waiting."[4] When it comes to our sexuality, playing by God's rules is the best way to win the game.

Sex is a normal drive. Why not act on it?

Without question, the sexual expression between a man and a woman (within marriage) was one of God's greatest gifts to human beings. And, yes, it is a normal drive. Unlike animals, however, humans share more than genitals. Sexual intercourse fuses our physical bodies with our very spirit. This powerful combination of body and soul produces a volatile drive that must be properly managed.

Dr. Archibald Hart, dean of the Graduate School of Psychology at Fuller Seminary, says the intensity of the sex drive for many men "feels like a volcano. Explosive and unpredictable, it continues to burn deep down in the groin, even when there's no reason for it. It may lay dormant for a while, only grumbling occasionally. But it awakens sooner or later." Given its intensity, Dr. Hart cautions that our sex drive "can lay waste to everything in its path including

> **Unlike animals, however, humans share more than genitals.**

honor, reputation, families, virginity, fidelity, chastity, good intentions, lifelong promises, and spiritual commitments."[5]

I recall a dinner party where the topic of this book was mentioned. One non-Christian lady remarked, "Bob, I imagine your position is that it's okay to satisfy the sex drive as long as you practice safe sex?" On the contrary, I explained my writing reflects my personal experience—save sex for marriage. Astounded, she asked, "But why don't you act on your sex drive now?"

Since she wasn't a born-again Christian, I didn't think she would accept the advice of the apostle Paul. He wrote, "each of you should learn to control his own body in a way that is holy and honorable" (1 Thess. 4:4). Rather, I explained that I may have an urge—a drive—to buy a Lexus. Or maybe it's nothing quite that extravagant. It might be as simple as a drive to eat a jumbo bag of nacho potato chips. Just because I have an urge doesn't mean I'm powerless to control it.

All of life requires restraint. I'm puzzled why so few have the inner strength to exercise some small measure of discipline when it comes to their sexuality. How about you? Do you have the fortitude to go the distance? Would you even *want* to go the distance?

What's wrong with premarital sex between consenting people? It doesn't hurt anybody.

Whenever someone lobs that line at me, I feel like saying, "Get real, pal!" What about the inevitable sexually transmitted disease—many of which have no cure? What of pregnancy and the temptation to abort public embarrassment through the murder of a newly placed life in the womb? How about the emotional trauma of giving away a part of one's very spirit, only to have the partner forget your phone number in the morning? That's reality, and reality holds more pain than joy when sex is engaged in before saying "I do."

For me, it wasn't necessarily the aforementioned "fears" associated with casual sex. Rather, it was the spiritual dimension that stuck in my brain. In college, I learned premarital sex is a violation of the "marriage covenant" set forth by God. A *what*? Hang in there with me for a minute.

A covenant is much like our modern-day contract. My

biblical history professor spent several days discussing with us the meaning of a covenant. There are basically two kinds of covenants used in the Bible: between equal parties and between a sovereign and his subject.

When a covenant is arranged between equals, they can negotiate their treaty any way they like. However, in the second kind of covenant, the sovereign determines the terms. He does so without question. His reasoning is final. And typically the sovereign lists the blessings and consequences if and when the covenant is honored or violated.

Interestingly, every biblical covenant usually features an outward symbol to serve as a reminder of the covenant. For example, God promised us that he would never again destroy humankind with a flood. The Lord says, "Whenever the rainbow appears in the clouds, I will see it and remember the everlasting covenant between God and all living creatures of every kind on the earth" (Gen. 9:16).

Perhaps this may come as news to you, but in Genesis 17:10, God selected *circumcision* as a sign of his covenant with man. At this point in my college studies, I had to ask the obvious question—why circumcision? Why not pierce our nose or cut off a piece of earlobe? My insightful professor—with his somewhat twisted sense of humor—explained: "Fellows, God wanted to remind you on a daily basis that every aspect of creation is to be governed by his decree . . . even your penis."

I guess that means if I were to engage in casual sex, I'd be meddling with the covenant! And that's not a casual idea.

No guy can wait until marriage, so why not practice safe sex?

Again, the notion that *no* guy or girl can exhibit sexual restraint until the wedding vows have been uttered is simply untrue. Amy Grant waited. Super model Rachel Fisk waited. Actor Kirk Cameron waited. As of this writing, *L.A.*

Law attorney Jane Halliday is a virgin. So concerned about their commitment to chastity, the Christian rap group D.C. Talk penned a song pledging to wait. You better sit down for this bit of news—even the king of morally-warped television, Phil Donahue, was a virgin as he went to the altar for his first marriage.

What about safe sex?

I wish I could introduce you to a sixteen-year-old girl, let's call her Stephanie. I met Stephanie in Sacramento at a youth convention where she was preparing to tell her story. Evidently, this Christian young woman embraced the safe sex myth and had sexual intercourse *one time*. She "played" by the Planned Parenthood rule book and carefully used a brand new condom.

When I saw her, she was seven months pregnant.

Real life situations like these have prompted many condom advertisers to rephrase the expression "safe sex" to "*safer* sex." Even if condom manufacturers one day invent a 100-percent effective prophylactic, there will never be a condom that can protect my mind from unwanted memories. Further, no condom has the ability to protect my heart from the loss of self-esteem that inevitably follows a cheap, one-night stand.

> **There will never be a condom that can protect my mind from unwanted memories.**

A.C. Green shoots straight when he asserts, "It's a lie to say that putting a condom on makes you as secure as Fort Knox. Condoms have a hard enough time just stopping a woman from getting pregnant, let alone blocking an HIV virus, which is 450 times smaller than sperm itself. It's like water going through a net."[6] Practice safe sex? No thank you. I believe we should work to "Save Sex."

What Ever Happened to Cooties?

Do you remember cooties? That fatal childhood affliction was transferred by the simple touch of a member of the opposite sex. Cooties were both gross and dangerous. If you had 'em, friends would not allow you to play on their kickball team for at least twenty-four hours. One thing is sure, cooties certainly kept the boys and girls a safe distance apart. In the nineties, it will take much more than the imaginary bogeyman of cooties to keep you from wandering into the garden of sensual delights. Why? If you make a commitment to honor the Lord with your body—to treat the gift of virginity (or second virginity) with loving care and respect, that decision will, in most cases, not be reinforced by what you see on television or at the movies, or by what you hear in popular music.

For example, over the last twelve years of speaking to youth, I've challenged thousands of teenagers to name *just one song* that they have heard on Top 40 radio that says, in effect, waiting to have sex until marriage is a good idea—a noble idea, or even a possibility.

To sweeten the deal, I'll offer a twenty-dollar reward if they can name *one* song. (Can you think of one?) To date, nobody has been able to identify such a tune (on secular radio). As far as my research goes, there has never been a song in the Top 40 applauding virginity. (Although it didn't receive any air play, "Keep It in Your Pants" by rap artist Young M.C. leaned in that direction.)

Since modern media doesn't provide any of the reinforcement necessary to sustain a desire to live the chaste life, how will you and I stay on track? I'm confident chapter 6 will be an invaluable resource to strengthen your resolve.

Button Your Fly

Several years ago, I was leading a discussion about music with fourth graders at a Christian school. With an embarrassed giggle, one youngster asked if Madonna's hit song "Like a Virgin" was good or bad. Unsure how much students in fourth grade knew about sex, I asked the class to define "virgin" for me.

Sally said, "It's a girl who doesn't do sex." I see. "Can boys be virgins, too?" I inquired. In one of those priceless moments, with hand outstretched Mark exclaimed, "I am, I am!" I wish I had that on videotape. My first thought was that only in the fourth grade would a boy proudly wear such a label. In fact, as I've traveled around the world, I've occasionally mentioned from stage that by God's grace, and obedience to his Word, I am still a virgin at my age. It saddens—and angers me—when an older single pulls me aside to whisper a "confession": "Bob, I'm a virgin, too. I can't believe I'm *not* the only one." What kind of a world do we live in? When someone makes a commitment to virginity, we should applaud them! Instead, we treat them as some kind of monstrosity.

What advice might I give that little fourth grade young man regarding future sexual decisions? The admonition of the apostle Paul to Timothy is the best guiding light I could offer. Paul writes, "Cling tightly to your faith in Christ and always keep your conscience clear, doing what you know is right. For some people have disobeyed their consciences and have deliberately done what they knew was wrong. It isn't surprising that soon they lost their faith in Christ after defying God like that" (1 Tim. 1:19 LB).

Tested by Fire

I'm a sexual being. So are you. It's possible you might be feeling this intellectual and biblical discussion sounds good *on paper*. But on Friday night, such conversation falls three letters short of a full alphabet: S-E-X. I've been there and know what you're feeling—actually, I'm still there! And what's particularly maddening is that all of my life I've made a commitment to "seek first his kingdom." To do things *his* way, even when *I* may have written a different script.

Take the challenge of Matthew 6:25, "Do not worry about your life, what you will eat or drink; or about your body, what you will wear." Although Jesus doesn't specifically mention marriage, it seems clear the sacrament of marriage would be among the concerns he wants us to cease worrying about and trust him.

In fact, several verses later the Lord adds, "So do not worry, saying, 'What shall we eat?' or 'What shall we drink?' or 'What shall we wear?' For the pagans run after all these things, and your heavenly Father knows that you need them" (Matt. 6:31–32).

Oh, yeah? He knows my desire for a spouse? You mean, my file didn't blow off of his desk? He's truly aware of my need for intimacy and desire for sexual expression? Then why doesn't God *answer* my prayers (and those of my entire family tree) and do something! I've heard women friends expressing frustration over their intense desire to bear children. Evidently, the pressure they feel to get on with motherhood tends to make their biological clock sound more like Big Ben.

Let's be honest, dear reader. If you've been single any length of time, those thoughts do tend to flood the mind. Why? Because it seems that "if God loves me, why am I *still* single?" is a fair question. In some ways, the knowledge that God (1) is aware of our desire for a spouse and sexual intimacy; (2) has promised to provide for *all* of our needs; yet (3) still hasn't acted on our behalf, only compounds our frustration. This realization easily robs us of our inner peace and confidence in God's ability to provide.

> **If God loves me, why am I still single?**

Given this emotional and spiritual tug-of-war, why have I chosen to wait to have sex for thirty-seven years? Ah, and why should *you* begin, or continue, to wait? More importantly, as one confidante asked, "Bob, how'd ya manage to keep your fiery Grecian hormones in check?" That's the million-dollar question. As you'll see momentarily, the answer boils down to these four principles:

- Marriage and sex should *not* be our objective—rather, becoming a godly lover is the goal.

- Instead of seeking sexual fulfillment, cultivate the fine art of intimacy.

- Recognize that emotions are like a drunk driver. Our emotional cycle will invariably attempt to push our sex drive off of the moral high road.

- Learn how to be an awesome, godly lover from those who are doing it right. (Hint: few marriages in Hollywood qualify.)

As promised, the following pages provide a sensible strategy to help us prepare ourselves to experience deep intimacy now and dynamic sex at such time that the Lord brings a spouse our way.

CHAPTER 2

Sex and Intimacy: Listening to Those Who Are Married

I don't like the institution of marriage. I don't think it's good for women. And I don't think any woman should ever get married. So, I just have to say, don't get married; just live with a guy and, ya know, if he starts actin' up, then just dump him.

—*Roseanne Barr*[1]

Let him kiss me with the kisses of his mouth— for your love is more delightful than wine.

—*Song of Songs 1:2*

I have a fear.

The longer I wait to experience the gift of sex, the more time I have to wonder, "Will I be a good sexual partner when I get married?" Behind that question lies a deeper apprehension, "Will I be able to satisfy my wife so that she will never pick the passion fruit of another lover?"

Evidently, for Roseanne Barr marriage resembled an endurance contest. A battle of the wills. Not so for Solomon. He and his bride celebrated an ongoing feast of passion. They couldn't get enough of each other!

So, what accounts for great sex?

Even though I'm single, I'd still like to know what is required to be an awesome lover. Why, you ask, is that important, since marriage most likely lies somewhere off in the distant future? Look at it this way. No one prepares to compete in the Olympics the night before. The wisest athletes spend *years* in training. Given the absurdly high rate of divorce, if I want my marriage to go the distance, I better give it a running start. And since most of us singles have an improperly defined picture of what makes for satisfying intimacy, there's a lot of work to be done!

That's why *now*—not after the wedding vows are spoken—is the best time for you and me to get a jump on some answers.

So what makes for great sex?

That depends on who you listen to.

> **Most of us singles have an improperly defined picture of what makes for satisfying intimacy.**

Taken for a Ride

It was a cool evening as I traveled on highway 95 in southern Florida. Scanning my radio dial I was looking for something to warm up the trip home—and got more than I bargained for. I bumped into a program on WIOD 610 AM called, "Passion Phone." The show was hosted by the heavy-breathing Erin Somers (no doubt an alias).

Although a married woman, Somers wanted to explore the seedy side of sex with her radio audience. The question burning in her loins that evening was group sex. Throughout the show, she repeated her mantra: "Twice the pleasure with half of the work." Dialing with sweaty palms, callers phoned in their alleged trysts—some incestuous, some in public places. Throughout the program, Somers played the role of sultry cheerleader.

At one point, a caller explained her interest in a foursome. Somers responded, "Oh, cool." Where does one pick up all of these extra partners? Somers proposed three options: a friend, an associate, or even a complete stranger. Not having my portable tape recorder with me, I made copious notes as they conversed about the wonders of group copulation.

Somers: Which do you prefer, a threesome or foursome?

Caller: Either one. My girlfriend and I are ready to go. Hey, it's the nineties!

"Yeah, bonehead!" I shouted at my car radio. "Get a clue." At no other time in history has the very core of civilization been threatened because of such stupid suicidal behavior!

Caller: My girlfriend and I are planning a threesome with a transvestite.

Somers: Wow! Call back and let us know how it works out!

Does she mean call back from the AIDS ward?

Caller: I was doing my girlfriend when her mom came into the room. I was all nervous that she'd be mad.

Somers: What happened?

Caller: Instead of freaking out, her mom joined in! As it turned out, I married the mother. Now, we both want to do the group sex thing again with her daughter.

No boundaries, no limits? Does such sickness make for dynamic sex? It sounds like these folks are just bored with themselves. After all, they probably know more about their neighborhood grocer than the partner lying next to them in their bed. Where's the long-term satisfaction in that?

I hate to pop Erin's prophylactic (she made a passing reference to using a condom), but the AIDS virus is 450 times smaller than sperm—which the best condoms properly used only block eighty-five percent of the time. How effective will they be with this killer disease?

One thing is clear. Singles who pursue the kind of bizarre, casual pleasures Somers celebrates *cannot* possibly enjoy sex in the fullest sense of the word because, as we'll read in a moment, such behavior is outside of God's design.

Likewise, some Christian singles may be repulsed by this kind of sexual free-for-all, but don't think there's anything wrong sleeping with their long-term boyfriend or girlfriend. Worse, engaged couples may rationalize that they're getting married anyway so why not grab a little action before they walk the aisle?

All of these sexual expressions—regardless of the rationale—fall short of God's design and will cause us pain if we engage in them. The apostle Paul puts it this way: "Flee from sexual immorality. All other sins a man commits are outside his body, but he who sins sexually sins against his own body" (1 Cor. 6:18).

They probably know more about their neighborhood grocer than the partner lying next to them in their bed.

To help us properly understand what truly makes for great sex, this chapter will draw upon the perspectives of those who are faithfully married. Why? As I mentioned in the previous chapter, the answer to our quest lies in this principle: Learn how to be an awesome, godly lover from those who are doing it *right*. Here we go.

Beautiful Payoffs

There's an old story about a newlywed couple. One night after making love, the young husband threw his pants at his bride. With a snobbish flare he said, "Try them on." She answered, "You know they'll never fit me." "You got it," he snorted. With his ego in high gear, the naive bridegroom blasted, "Never forget who wears the pants in this house!"

With a piercing stare, the bride plucked her panties from the bed and tossed them at her husband. "Go ahead, try them on," she demanded. "No way! I'll never get into these!" Heading to the bathroom, she coldly remarked, "Yes, and until your attitude changes, that's absolutely right!"

This poor lad never learned what it *really* takes to wear the pants in the house. Unless he's a fast study, his sex and intimacy in that marriage will be in the doghouse for a long time.

Not desiring to make the same mistake as this sorry chap, I quizzed a number of friends whose marriages I respected. Some were newlyweds. Others tied the knot eight, fifteen, even forty-plus years ago. All of them were Christian couples working on their first marriage. I found their insight absolutely incredible—primarily because of how basic and practical their advice was. No tabloid sizzling headlines here like "Amazing Sexual Revelation from a Martian Seen Speaking with the President."

Just plain, biblically-based common sense.

Okay, for the last time, "What makes for great sex?"

Two things. These veterans informed me that (1) a right relationship with the Lord, and (2) healthy intimacy expressed between husband and wife lie at the heart of my quest. Although technique is an important factor, time and time again I would be told that these two ingredients serve as *the* foundational building block for the best sex God designed for humans to enjoy.

Yikes! How, then, would they define intimacy?

Dynamic intimacy within marriage is the exchange, usually through rich conversation or mutual activity, that *draws two people together* and fosters intense closeness and personal satisfaction. It requires time, demands openness, and by

Graduates of the Madonna school of sex may know how the parts go together, but they can't get beyond the one-dimensional exhibition stage.

nature obligates each person to be disarmed and vulnerable. Sometimes intimacy is stimulated by a crisis. More often it's the sharing of one's hopes, dreams, and deepest longings that nurtures the growth of marital intimacy.

Graduates of the Madonna school of sex may know how the parts go together, but they can't get beyond the one-dimensional exhibition stage. As a couple expresses this oneness of spirit, their sexual expression takes them to a wonderfully new dimension. No longer is it a mere freak show attended by strangers.

Putting-In Instead of Putting-Out

I've always disliked the expression "putting-out." My friends in public high school would use it to describe a girl who gave them what they wanted—sexually speaking. Far too many singles never graduate from those high school ways. Instead, in their desire to be accepted by a member of the opposite sex, they expend significant levels of energy putting-out—sexually, emotionally, or financially.

Maybe you've played that game—or are still playing it. Yet deep down you feel like there's got to be a more constructive approach. There is! Use the season of singleness to grow into the best person you can possibly be. Put in, not out. Invest in who you are *becoming*. You'll be in a better position to attract and enjoy the spouse you're praying for.

And, risking redundancy, we should learn how to be an awesome, godly lover from those who are doing it right. To help us move in that direction, I surveyed a number of married couples, asking them this question: If you could do it over, what would you have done differently *before* marriage to enhance intimacy on the other side of the altar. Five items found their way to the top. They recommended:

1. Change your approach to dating.
2. Practice guarding your thought life.
3. Save sex for marriage.
4. Learn how to navigate lonely times alone.
5. Be a better communicator.

I must admit, as my married friends provided me with this list, I didn't immediately see the connection between these items and growing into a great lover. My younger brother Steve (married ten years) helped me out. He said, "The expression godly 'lover' tends to denote something relatively sexual. So much of life within marriage is nonsexual, yet intricately *related* to sexual intimacy." And prior to marriage is the time to establish good habits.

> Invest in who you are becoming. You'll be in a better position to attract and enjoy the spouse you're praying for.

As we work through the list, let's be realistic. These five tips will take *time* to master. There are no shortcuts. No magic pills. But for those singles who have the fortitude to forge ahead, I'm confident the payoffs down the road will be simply beautiful. Let's examine each recommendation one at a time.

1. Change your approach to dating.

Scores of books have been written on appropriate dating habits for singles. I've noticed there are primarily three models to choose from: dating on a one-on-one basis, dating in groups, or no dating—just hang out and get to know folks in small-group settings. Regardless of the approach you subscribe to, there's the underlying matter of *agenda*.

Many married respondents admitted they played the

dating game with wrong, self-serving motives. In a word, they subscribed to the secular dating model: each person seeks primarily his or her self-interest within a romantic setting; each person asks, "What can I *get* from my date?"

Learn how to be an awesome, godly lover from those who are doing it right.

Like traffic on the opposite side of the street, the Christian's agenda for dating ought to be headed in a radically different direction. "What can I *give*?" or "How can I enhance the other person?" should be our focus when we date. My father, who assists with a large singles ministry and has been married for forty-four years, believes that "many Christian singles consider that approach naive, unrealistic, and undesirable." In fact, he observes far too many are embracing the secular model.

Here's the message from the married perspective: Be careful not to date and mate with the manipulative "what can I get" agenda. It's an ugly quality—especially inside of marriage. Instead, Ephesians 5:25 should set the standard: "Husbands, love your wives, just as Christ loved the church and *gave himself up* for her" [emphasis added].

For example, Grace confided that it took her eleven years of marriage before she got a handle on her tendency to manipulate her husband for the things—especially clothing—that she desired. She traced her well-tested routine back to her dating days. If she wanted something, Grace "pushed the right buttons" to get it. But, Grace explained, she felt so empty inside because she knew her husband was only loving her or treating her special on an artificial level.

At forty-six, Frank, who attended a Promise Keepers convention in Denver, said he finally began to understand the concept of giving unselfishly of himself to his wife. Although excited about this new approach, Frank felt saddened that he had wasted sixteen years of marriage pursuing selfish goals. Grabbing my arm with firm resolve, Frank impressed upon me the importance of beginning to cultivate unconditional love *now* in my dating relationships.

2. Practice guarding your thought life.

Back in high school, my friend Don and I would often hang out by the loading dock at lunch. It was fascinating to watch this new believer fight with his "old man" regarding lusty thoughts. On several occasions, a drop-dead, seriously gorgeous coed would strut past us. Don's eyes would follow her curves as closely as a Corvette hugs the road. He'd turn and tell me, "Bob, she 'ministers' to my eyes!"

If lusting after every good-looking man or woman dominates your mind as a single, you'll forever be comparing—and degrading—your mate after marriage. There are numerous consequences to an unchecked thought life. Sue reflected, "It's so tempting to slip into a pattern of fantasizing about someone other than your life-long love." Which, she confessed, "was the first step toward my marital dissatisfaction and infidelity."

Although Andrew attended a Christian college in the South, he constantly made excuses for his fixation with the female form. In fact, using an off-campus post office box, Andy subscribed to *Playboy* during his college years. Presently thirty-nine and married with several children, Andy admits that habit was an incredibly tough one to break—even after he got married. Andy explained: "Just because you get married doesn't mean your mind will suddenly relinquish its interest in the seedy side of sex. I wish I hadn't fed my mind with that trash," he adds.

In Matthew 5:27–28, Jesus warned: "You have heard that it was said, 'Do not commit adultery.' But I tell you that anyone who looks at a woman lustfully has already committed adultery with her in his heart." I'll be the first to admit

If lusting after every good-looking man or woman dominates your mind as a single, you'll forever be comparing—and degrading—your mate after marriage.

that guarding the theater of my mind is a *daily* priority. And it's certainly not easy.

So on a practical level, whenever my single friends would ogle a "foxy babe," I'd ask myself a question: "What am I supposed to do with that information?" I'd force myself to focus on a more productive use of my brain space. I'm not always successful in my attempt to keep the retina from roving, but that doesn't stop me from trying to do what the Lord would have me do by practicing restraint.

3. Save sex for marriage.

Allan, a married friend in his fifties, once whispered to me, "It's good to find a woman who believes in waiting to have sex *before* marriage. The key is to find one who believes in sex *after* marriage!" I've heard many war stories about this or that person's lack of a sex life now that they're married. You've probably heard a few, too. The impact of such tales can be to "get all you can *now* before it's too late."

I could fill a book with stories of regret—married couples whose sex life is plagued by past lovers. Rachel tells me, "Every night I'd pray that the Lord would remove memories of past sexual encounters. It just ruins our intimacy." Scott, a former stud of the nightclub, agrees. Now a Christian, he admits, "Not only did sexual sin separate me from God when I was single, it haunts me like a bad dream now that he has graciously given me a lovely bride."

Abstaining from premarital sex is not just good advice from those who are presently married, it's also what we're asked to do by God. Paul, Silas, and Timothy express-mailed a letter to the church at Thessalonica. Their urgent message: "It is God's will that you should be sanctified; that you should avoid sexual immorality; that each of you should learn to control his own body in a way that is holy and honorable, not in passionate lust like the heathen, who do not know God" (1 Thess. 4:3–5).

If you have lost your virginity but desire to honor Christ in the future, I'd offer two things. First, be mature enough to accept the consequences of your behavior. Don't minimize what you've done and learn to avoid circumstances that contribute to compromise (see chapter 6). At the same time, be quick to embrace the knowledge that you can stand clean before the Savior.

How? Accept the forgiveness Jesus has to offer you. Read this verse and pin it to your mirror: "If we confess our sins, he is faithful and just and will forgive us our sins and purify us from all unrighteousness" (1 John 1:9).

Afterward, make a pledge to the Lord, your future

PEANUTS reprinted by permission of United Feature Syndicate, Inc.

spouse, and to yourself that you will remain faithful from now on. I fully recognize that this kind of pledge, coupled with the Lord's kindness, prevented me from prematurely unwrapping this breathtaking gift. Our best efforts to abstain—apart from God's direct protective covering—are simply not enough. We must lean on him.

4. Learn how to navigate lonely times alone.

It's a fact. Many married people report numerous occasions when they desired sexual intimacy at the end of the day, but their spouse fell asleep. No warm embrace, not even a conversation. Although you're together, you're still alone. But wait a minute! I thought only singles experienced solitude. Now what? Do you flick on the TV for company? If the truth be known I'd bet that a primary reason why David Letterman and Jay Leno have such massive late-night audiences is due to the fact that millions of lonely married people are tuned in.

It is downright naive to believe that marriage or sex will be the solution to our loneliness. If you and I are often melancholy as singles, we will likely be unhappy when sex is lying right next to us. I've found it helpful to become my own best friend. Considering the fact that I have to live with myself for the rest of my life, that's not such a bad idea! Truthfully, it works.

> It is downright naive to believe that marriage or sex will be the solution to our loneliness.

I like me. I thoroughly enjoy my own company. Sounds conceited? Hardly. When we remember we're *not* a half of a person that magically becomes a whole person upon marriage, we learn to love ourselves—even in singlehood.

Do feelings of loneliness strike? Absolutely. I use those times to reflect, to write letters, or to get lost in a gripping novel. I might add that it's terrific preparation for the inevitable quiet nights of marriage. Sure beats watching the tube. After all, I hate those endless commercials for "Press On Nails" that dominate late-night television.

5. Be a better communicator.

For many years I penned a column on music and popular entertainment for two Focus on the Family magazines, *Brio* for girls and *Breakaway* for guys. When all was said and done, I probably read more than ten thousand letters from teen readers. You know, I observed a fascinating dynamic. When a girl would ask me a question, it was usually animated, packed with many little details—not to mention a plethora of words. Some questions went on for three pages, punctuated by colorful ink, cute stickers, smiley faces, and hearts.

The guys? We're talking a two-sentence question— max. Get to the point. No chummy stickers.

From New York to Norway, Los Angeles to Latin America, guys universally spoke the same language: brevity. Granted, there were a few noteworthy exceptions. But on the whole, the boys were men of few words. (I might add that the males tended to be more expressive when in sharp disagreement with me. Anger seemed to produce an abundant supply of harsh words, and at times forceful art.)

The sparse use of words in communication might do the job when you're twelve. But inside of a marriage, it's the formula for disaster. The same goes for the woman who has the inability to "get to the point before Christmas," as one man put it.

How can you polish your communication skills? Put your hands on a copy of *Men Are from Mars, Women Are from Venus* by Dr. John Gray. You'll laugh and, more importantly, you'll learn practical ways to nurture this important ingredient to intimacy.

Breakfast in Bed

You've probably heard the advice to married coupls: sex begins in the kitchen. In other words, if a husband and wife desire to set the stage for sexual expression at night, they would be wise to begin the process throughout the day. A flirtatious look. A gentle touch. A soft-spoken secret. These gestures move them toward a physical expression of their lifelong commitment.

For the single, I contend that intimacy doesn't have to wait for the kitchen. Although the sexual aspect will be delayed until later, learning how to be intimate begins now. Our conversation in the next chapter will focus on intimacy for men and women, and why it's often shallow. And we'll look at the matter of intimacy through the eyes of the One who designed it.

Incidentally, at the outset of this chapter I mentioned an apprehension: "Will I be able to satisfy my wife so that she will never pick the passion fruit of another lover?" A resounding *yes!* sounds as I rely upon God's grace, and practice the principles found in the balance of this book.

CHAPTER 3

The Fine Art of Intimacy

Intimacy, fulfilling, enjoyable, meaningful
intimacy must emerge from the God-ordained
context of commitment and acceptance and
marital harmony. That's all part of his arrangement. The original design cannot be improved
upon, even though the propaganda sings
another tune.

—*Charles Swindoll[1]*

Sex is, in fact, often used as an excuse for actually avoiding intimacy.

—*Dr. Gabrielle Brown[2]*

In March of 1993, Americans were shocked to learn the news from Lakewood, California. On the surface, Lakewood was a modest little community of 74,000 residents. But beneath the well-groomed landscaping there brewed a sex scandal that sent tremors across the nation. Nine well-known athletes, ages fifteen to eighteen, were arrested and sent to jail. Their alleged crime? The sexual assault, molestation, and rape of girls under age seventeen. One instance included a mere child, aged ten.

They called themselves the Spur Posse—named after their favorite basketball team, the San Antonio Spurs. But unlike their pro-ball heroes, these juvenile delinquents scored one "point" each time they had sex with a different 51 girl. Rather than a gang, the Spurs saw themselves as a "group of friends" with a common interest—sex.

Twenty-year-old Dana Belman is the self-acclaimed founder of the Spur Posse. In rather crude terms, Dana explains the circumstances leading up to the formation of their deviant club: "See, in Lakewood you'll have a girl-friend, and then, next thing you know, either your brother or your best friend's f—ed her, so it's like d—. So then all our friends just thought of girls as nothing but a point."[3]

Word on the street says he's collected sixty-three to date.

While wolfing down a Nacho Supreme for lunch at Taco Bell, posse member Eric Richardson defended his buddy's actions. "They pass out condoms, teach sex education and pregnancy-this and pregnancy-that," the seventeen-year-old said while kissing his girlfriend. "But they don't teach us any rules."[4] No guilt. No remorse. Just the facts.

Dana was asked by a reporter what the difference is between good and bad sex. The posse's guru reflected, "There's never bad sex for a guy." Oh, really? Offering a word of clarification, Dana added, "There is bad sex when a girl's breath's kicking."[5] Bad breath?

While many communities cross-examined their leading athletes searching for signs of sexual impropriety, Holly-wood was calculating a way to make a quick buck. Mike Weber, sporting a lean well-conditioned body, boasted that Hollywood desired to make a movie centered around his life. The only justification Weber offers for his exploits: "Any guy is going to love to have sex. If you have to throw a line or two to get it, you're going to do it."[6]

How satisfying are their encounters? In a passing moment of honest reflection, Dana confesses: "It kinda gets boring sometimes, you know, just like going over to a girl's house when you don't even care about her, no feelings, and you just throw a couple of pumps, and you're done, and you just go back home."[7] Don Juan he's not.

What's Love Got to Do with It?

In spite of the Posse's many sexual conquests, few would label these derelicts as good lovers. With well-tanned, well-toned bodies they've certainly got the *look*—if only they had a clue. It's a case of athletic boys trying to do an end-run around God's design for marital intimacy. They've grabbed for the gusto now, but in the long term will wind up out of the game.

As the saying goes, "boys will be boys"—a notion I absolutely detest. What's sad is the amazing number of men who still adhere to such boyish practices. Why? For one, we have few good examples of appropriate displays of affection. It seems men are programmed to associate sex as something you *do*, rather than an extension of who you *are*. As a result, sex becomes the *goal*—while sharing one's soul takes a backseat.

I might add that a significant number of women play along. To satisfy their longing for love and intimacy, they willingly settle for sex as a cheap substitute. Genuine intimacy appears to be so evasive. The lonely woman might reason, "Tonight I'm by myself, again. Am I *that* undesirable?" All of a sudden, the idea of being noticed at a dance club by some hunk (with a partially unbuttoned shirt and gold chain dangling onto his pecs) makes her heart skip a beat.

> **Men are programmed to associate sex as something you do, rather than an extension of who you are ... sex becomes the goal—while sharing one's soul takes a backseat.**

For men and women alike, far too often we're tempted to view sex as an external "fix"—if not a shortcut—to gratify our internal longings. And it's a sick game where the players use sexual conquest to define their identity. In the process, participants lose opportunities to fully enter into the golden fields of intimate exchange.

I desire more than a passing imitation of intimacy, don't you? Let's set a higher standard. Our ultimate objective? As singles, we should *cultivate the fine art of intimacy and leave the immature (and unfulfilling) conquest game-playing to the dead-end club scene*. If we do, you and I will enjoy rich rewards in our relationships today, and be in the best position to maximize marital intimacy down the road.

I assure you the rewards are worth the effort.

Designer Genes

Shortly after creating Adam, the Lord made this startling assessment: "It is not good for the man to be alone. I will make a helper suitable for him" (Genesis 2:18). Alone? I thought Adam had a jungle full of fuzzy animal buddies. You know, his own private zoo.

Why did the Lord make this observation?

There's a difference between company and companionship. You enjoy company; you share your soul with a companion. Adam had loads of company. But . . . sharing a quiet afternoon with a zebra? Even a talking parrot has a limited vocabulary. (Speaking of which, my two blue and gold macaw parrots are more conversant than some dates I've had.) But I can assure you they're no substitute for human conversation.

The Lord knew Adam needed a soul mate. Let's reread his situation:

> "It is not good for the man to be alone. I will make a helper suitable for him.". . . So the man gave names to all the livestock, the birds of the air and all the beasts of the field. But for Adam no suitable helper was found. So the LORD God caused the man to fall into a deep sleep; and while he was sleeping, he took one of the man's ribs and closed up the place with flesh. Then the LORD God made

a woman from the rib he had taken out of the man, and he brought her to the man. (Gen. 2:18, 20–22)

Here, then, is our starting point: intimacy, sex, and marriage were designed by God. As Designer, the Lord constructed a genetic code of intimacy which he wove deep into the heart and soul of Adam. However, my emphasis here is not Adam's felt need, but God's design to satisfy his heart's longing. Sadly, it appears that many today are attempting to fill their need for intimacy through various experiences and stimulants—other than the course set by God. Whether a member of the Spur Posse, a guy who frequents a strip joint, or perhaps a woman who seeks attention at the meat market dance club, these affairs of the heart are a cheap substitute for God's original design.

> **Leave the immature (and unfulfilling) conquest game-playing to the dead-end club scene.**

Have you ever taken the time to step back and consider how radically God's design for intimacy differs from the Posse-type juvenile or the dance club snake? This viper slithers through the crowd looking for an easy catch. He, like you and me, has the same God-given need for intimacy. Yet rather than get on board with the Designer's program, he seeks a quick solution or temporary fix for the longing inside.

As we cultivate the fine art of intimacy, review with me our definition of dynamic intimacy:

- It's an exchange—not a one-sided activity
- Requires time
- Demands openness
- Obligates both parties to be disarmed and vulnerable
- Rich conversation or mutual activity deepens it
- Can be stimulated by a crisis

- Draws two people together
- Hopes, dreams, and deepest longings are freely shared
- Fosters closeness and personal satisfaction

Permit me to be completely black-and-white for a minute. When it comes to our pursuit of intimacy, we have two—and only two—options: God's way or the human way. And just as the North is different from the South, these approaches are polar opposites. Like oil and water, God's way and the human way simply do not mix.

There's no middle ground.

You can probably guess what I mean by God's way— especially in light of our working definition of intimacy. So what do I mean by "the human way"? Think back to the wildly popular television series "Cheers." Remember Ted Danson's character Sam Malone? Sam was the ultimate womanizer. Using his self-serving charm and looks, Malone's only interest in a lady was the use of her body parts. Interestingly, the producers cast his sexual pursuits in a humorous light. He may have been lovable, but he couldn't have been farther from experiencing real intimacy if he tried.

Let's be honest. When it comes to intimacy, the human way looks very attractive on the surface. It's quicker. It's less costly, and it's surrounded by sizzling appeal. But as you'll see in the following chart, it doesn't measure up.

On the left, I've listed the attributes, challenges, and benefits awaiting those who seek to satisfy their intimacy needs as God would have them. The right side reveals the essence of the human approach. As you review these two lists, ask yourself, *Which approach to intimacy have I been taking in the past?*

Intimacy God's Way	Intimacy the Human Way
• Sacrificial	• Selfish
• Breeds happiness	• Breeds hardness of heart
• Requires time to mature	• Seeks immediate gratification
• Few good role models	• Numerous role models
• Demands determination	• Easier course to take
• Satisfies richly	• A temporary fix
• Free from guilt	• Plagued by guilt
• Relies upon spiritual	• Avoids spiritual
• Pleases God	• Angers God
• Real intimacy	• Counterfeit intimacy

"But wait, Bob," you might be thinking. "Before going much further, I'm *still* single, remember? What's this got to do with me?"

Here's the relevance.

It's easy for you and me to slip into bad habits—especially when it comes to our dating relationships. If we fail to cultivate the art of intimacy now, if we approach friendship, dating, and intimacy the human way, we'll lack the skills necessary for real intimacy in all relationships now—and especially down the road in marriage.

Take Larry. At forty-two, Larry is a good-looking, footloose bachelor. He made a commitment to Christ ten years ago and is heavily involved in church activities. But he's been through more than a dozen women since his conversion. Over dinner, Larry tells me how much he respects my ability to fulfill my intimacy needs God's way and wonders how I could possibly control myself.

As we ate, I couldn't help but observe his preoccupation with females: Our waitress walked past and his eyes followed her long legs. Likewise, the cute blond in the adjacent booth had him doing neck exercises throughout the meal. Larry admitted he loved "the ladies." Okay. Then why not just get with the program and settle down? "Are you kidding? I might meet somebody better," was the best he could come up with.

If we fail to cultivate the art of intimacy now ... we'll lack the skills necessary for real intimacy in all relationships—especially marriage.

Jumping in and out of relationships—not to mention bed—characterized Larry's level of intimacy. How sad. When it comes to relationships, Larry's idea of a concrete commitment would be signing his initials in wet cement. By his own admission, Larry's heart was growing cold—a by-product of seeking intimacy the human way.

"Larry," I felt like shouting, "quit microwaving all of your meals. Learn how to savor the rich aromas and deep flavors that the Crock-Pot has to offer!"

Laying My Foundation

There's a gorgeous waterway across the street from the condo where I'm writing these pages. Every morning I permit myself a refreshing jog. Today, I stopped to spend a few quiet moments on the dock. I wanted to find the answer to a nagging question I've been having: *Why do I approach sex and intimacy so differently?* Come to think of it, why am I so profoundly offended when I read headlines such as those surrounding the Spur Posse?

Further, upon what foundation did I build my understanding of sex and intimacy? Why was I enabled to stand strong—when my friends were tearing their clothing off faster than cars zoom across the German Autobahn?

A number of factors came to mind. As I recount my personal history, please believe me when I say I was not—*nor am I now*—a perfect, superhuman:

- I fell in love with Jesus as a young child.

- In answer to my parents' faithful prayers, I developed a desire to *always* please my heavenly Father. From childhood I began to pray this simple prayer: "Lord, help me to love what you love, and hate what you hate."

- As I grew, I'd ask the Lord to smile on my various endeavors. Proverbs 16:3 was my inspiration: "Ask the Lord to bless your plans, and you will be successful in carrying them out" (GOOD NEWS). Approaching the teen years, that prayer was expanded to include matters of sex and dating.

> Quit microwaving all of your meals. Learn how to savor the rich aromas and deep flavors that the Crock-Pot has to offer!

- I determined that if something I do does not bring joy to my heavenly Father, then regardless of the activity it shouldn't bring real joy to me. ("I have told you this so that *my* joy may be in you and that your joy may be complete," John 15:11 [emphasis added].)

- I came to believe that if you're not intimate with your heavenly Father, your earthly expressions of intimacy will fall short of what they could ultimately be.

- Since my mind is my most active sex organ, and in light of the scriptural command to control our minds, I worked to discipline my thoughts just as any athlete would discipline the body. ("That each of you should learn to control his own body in a way that is holy and honorable," 1 Thess. 4:4.)

- While at camp as a youngster, we had a guest speaker whose name I don't recall. His challenge I haven't forgotten: When you go on a date, treat her in the same fashion you'd want another guy to treat the woman who might one day become your wife.

- Regarding sex, the following verses formed my marching orders as a teenager. With this mandate inside of my head, imagine me trying to understand sexual intimacy apart from these passages.

Let us behave decently, as in the daytime, not in orgies and drunkenness, not in sexual immorality and debauchery, not in dissension and jealousy. Rather, clothe yourselves with the Lord Jesus Christ, and do not think about how to gratify the desires of the sinful nature. (Rom. 13:13–14)

Just when I thought I had it all together, the Lord sent me a friendly reminder not to get too cocky: "So, if you think you are standing firm, be careful that you don't fall!" (1 Cor. 10:12). In some ways, the Romans passage was the right hand of a matched pair of gloves. Peter held the left hand:

For *you have spent enough time* in the past *doing what pagans choose to do*—living in debauchery, lust, drunkenness, orgies, carousing and detestable idolatry. *They think it strange that you do not plunge with them* into the same flood of dissipation, and they heap abuse on you. But they will have to *give account* to him who is ready to judge the living and the dead. (1 Peter 4:3–5, emphasis added)

- Thankfully, I managed to avoid the general pagan mayhem Peter warns against. And I can attest from firsthand experience the apostle is so-o right—especially that part about unsaved friends who thought I was crazy for not joining into their free-for-all.

Reviewing this index of my personal journey, I noticed two building blocks that formed the foundation for my approach to sex and intimacy:

1. It is *unthinkable* to engage in sex without the knowledge that my first love—the Lord—is pleased.

2. It's impossible to share satisfying intimacy prior to marriage apart from being rooted in the Author of life.

Love Speaks

It's likely that you didn't have parents who displayed outward signs of intimate affection. In fact, as much as it might strike you as a wonderful idea, it's a tough one to picture. If you're like many of my friends, a nightly temper tantrum between your parents was typical. Lynnette told me growing up she used to frequently hear her folks scream, "Either you leave or I leave ... this relationship is nothing but hell!"

Throughout their forty-four years of marriage, my parents did a number of things to keep their friendship from becoming a battleground. It was easy to notice Mom and Dad using the little things to affirm and nourish their intimacy. I might add, they still continue to act like a pair of peach-faced love birds! Here are a few of my observations:

- Love notes frequently shared
- Large, hand-crafted posters celebrating their love
- Exchanged presents for no particular reason
- Public displays of affection: hugs, kisses, hand-holding
- Spoke numerous words of praise in the hearing of others
- Defended each other when others were critical
- Played piano, sang, and made beautiful music together
- Spent much time praying side-by-side on their knees
- Never publicly or privately bashed their spouse
- Practiced, "I'm sorry, will you forgive me?"
- Would be willing to forgive even when difficult to do
- Escaped for the weekend to an undisclosed nearby hotel

- Would engage in spontaneous worship with guitar in the middle of the night

No, the Cleavers' home was not next door. As a family, we had our portion of turbulence. My folks would be the first to admit that they had their share of disagreements. But overall the flight was amazingly smooth. What accounted for the steadiness of the trip? Dad wisely cultivated the fine art of intimacy with Mom. Perhaps he knew the old saying: "If mamma ain't happy, ain't nobody happy!" Ain't that the truth!

Intimate Apparel

Do you want to cultivate the fine art of intimacy? Great. Here's your homework assignment. Get intimate with Jesus. Share your hopes, dreams, and your heart's desires with him. Enjoy your good times with him—as well as the tough spots. Learn what pleases the Lord. Honor his desires. And ask him to make you a better lover of people. Be vulnerable with Jesus and admit your weaknesses.

He promises to take care of the rest! Believe me. I can attest to the fact that he does!

At this time, our study moves in an interesting direction. In the next chapter we'll examine the unique challenges of sex and intimacy for those previously married, yet single once again. Are you in that boat? If so, you face a number of unique dangers that can crash future plans for intimacy on the rocks of past failures. I'm looking forward to an eye-opening, hope-filled conversation!

But wait. A word to the single, never-wed crowd. Don't be tempted to breeze past—or just skim through—chapter 4. Who knows? Maybe the Lord's plan for you includes a blended family down the road. Whatever the future holds, studying the hurdles our "single-again" friends must overcome will be beneficial now—and conceivably invaluable later.

CHAPTER 4

Single, Again

Being divorced is like being hit by a Mack truck. If you live through it, you start looking very carefully to the right and to the left.

—*Jean Kerr, author*[1]

My grace is sufficient for you, for my power is made perfect in weakness.

—*Jesus, to Paul (2 Corinthians 12:9)*

*A*Mack truck, a freight train—it doesn't matter what caused the impact, the fact is you've been run over. Few experiences in life can adequately prepare one for such a crisis of the soul. Complicating your loss is the fact that your body's familiarity with touch and physical expressions of intimacy doesn't suddenly disappear.

A book on sex and intimacy for singles wouldn't be complete if it didn't include the challenges those who have been previously married but are single again encounter. I love the way my friend Sandra Aldrich described her predicament. Widowed at a young age, Sandra is quick to point out: "My husband may have died, but my hormones didn't die with him—they're very much alive!"

Ah, those crazy hormones. Many single-again individuals report they mistakenly confuse the need for a "healthy touch" with "sexual intercourse." For some, their newfound freedom propels them to explore excessive sexual expressions. The affirmation they seek and the longing to know they're still desirable catapults them headlong into the quagmire of regret.

We'll discover there's a better way.

Heartbreak Hotel

I confess that I face a disadvantage in our discussion. Although single, I have yet to sample the fruit from the "promised land." You won't find me pretending to know what it's like to lose my mate—whether through death or divorce. Through the years I've attempted to overcome this obstacle by becoming a better listener. Believe me, I've been listening.

As a public speaker for more than ten years, I've traveled extensively throughout North America. Across the miles, I've had numerous opportunities to meet and listen to others. Leaning across the fence, men and women have taken me into their confidence, sharing their painful stories as if we were next-door neighbors.

Listening has allowed me to better understand and feel more compassion for those who are single again—especially as it pertains to their sexual and intimate needs. The letter you're about to read is a true account of one such individual. I've selected it because it's well-suited to set the stage for this chapter.

> **Many single-again individuals report they mistakenly confuse the need for a "healthy touch" with "sexual intercourse."**

Meet "Stacey." This twenty-eight-year-old, vibrant young woman from Chicago has a solid career. She's educated and, I might add, a smart dresser. On the surface, Stacey's life would appear to be completely in order. Yet, as we're about to see, her world was turned upside down four long years ago.

I've taken the liberty to change the names, locations,

and dates in Stacey's letter to protect her privacy. Truthfully, those details are secondary to the issue at hand. It's a lengthy narrative, one that can't help but draw you in as she shares her story:

> At the age of twenty, I was wed to the man of my dreams. None of my family or friends would have guessed that my dream would take a nightmarish turn so quickly.
>
> I found myself at the ripe age of twenty-four sobbing profusely in a dark cold room realizing my "single, again" status. Honestly, it was a status I *never* wanted to experience. My eighteen-month-old daughter finally fell asleep after several hours of tossing and turning, crying from those unsettling baby thoughts. For the next few weeks I was to join her in those sleepless nights.
>
> A life without a husband who once was, a life without a father who was to be forever, a life of loneliness now stretched before me as far as the eye could see. I could imagine people secretly affixing their little labels on me: "Divorced," "Single—with a kid," "Untouchable."
>
> Bob, I pledged to Phil my undying love. I fully expected to spend all of my living days loving him, supporting his dreams—even looked forward to applying Ben Gay as we aged. All of a sudden, those days were over. How I longed for the intimacy I had grown so accustomed to sharing for four fantastic years.
>
> Being betrayed cut me to the core of my being.

Let me insert that those whose spouse is deceased often feel the same level of betrayal. Death, like divorce, short-changed their dreams and robbed them of their hope. Stacey continues:

> When I first met Phil, I was drawn to his self-confidence. I admired his adventurous and playful spirit. It wasn't long before we spent literally hours hiking, jet skiing—we even fished together. Our three-year friendship

was clearly headed for the altar. It was like a dream come true.

Phil treated me like a queen and was extremely generous. After we were wed, he continued to demonstrate these displays of his love. When we'd go skiing in Utah, he'd pick a cottage with a fireplace—and surprise me with a new snowsuit for the trip. Want to go camping? No problem. He'd buy brand-new gear.

Two years into the marriage, our son was born. Did Phil suddenly shift gears? No. Instead he lovingly provided fun treats for both little Timmy and me. Frankly, it seemed virtually every couple we knew envied us, and our new suburban home.

I paint such a pretty picture, Bob, because it *was* pretty. As far as I could tell, we did everything right. It was the American dream. Little did I know that all of Phil's generosity and loving attention from him was strictly out of guilt. He was having an affair all along— and I had no clue.

Looking back, I recall that my onetime best friend asked me an unusual question. Roxanne asked, "How much do you trust Phil?"

"Completely," I asserted. As it turned out, this former best friend was sleeping with *my* husband.

In my church, I saw marriage as a *sacrament*. The vows two people exchanged connected them as one flesh before the Creator. How anybody could walk away from such a contract with God was beyond me. From my point of view, I worked every day to be my husband's confidante, supporter, and best friend. I yearned to be the best wife a man could ever desire. Why was this so important to me? I didn't want to become a statistic.

And now I was.

After the divorce, I found myself wrestling with two questions: "What did I do wrong?" and "What did Roxanne have that I lacked?" My self-esteem was shot.

Stacey wrongly assumed that her lack of sexual experi-

ence was behind her husband's infidelity. Like many women
in her vulnerable position, she sought an inappropriate solution to this perceived inadequacy. Her remedy? Stacey
immediately threw herself into relationships based solely on
sex. Tossing caution aside caused further damage to her
aching heart. Worse, she picked up a sexually transmitted
disease in the process.

Break the Chains

Stacey's story tugs at my heart.

The first time I read her correspondence I wanted to
reach across the miles and give her a long, healthy hug.
Then I wanted to organize a SWAT team and put this bozo
Phil out of his misery. But for a Christian that, of course,
was not an option. (Instead, I prayed that God would put
things right!)

Stacey's account reminds me of a note from Gail. At
forty-two, Gail's husband Steve died unexpectedly from cancer. With three children, she figured nobody would find her
attractive. Lonely, depressed, and skeptical of her "mar-
ketability," Gail unknowingly became prey for vultures.

Enter Dean. You might call him Mr. Vulture personi-
fied. This old college buddy learned of Steve's death,
prompting him to get in touch. On the surface, Dean listened to Gail's worries and sympathized with her feelings.
But this bird of prey was just circling the sky, waiting for the
right moment of vulnerability to strike.

It took about a week.

In a moment of false security, you can probably guess
what happened. Gail engaged in sex with Dean. From her
perspective, it was a shortcut toward experiencing the intimacy she once had with her husband. Unbeknown to Gail,
for Dean it was "just another fling." Within a month this
affair lost its sizzle and he took off to find another victim. In

true vulture-like fashion, Dean left when the pickins were lean.

The temptation Stacey, Gail, and those who are now without a spouse face is to stop the leak in their emotional dam by plugging it with instant intimacy. As appealing as sexual contact may seem, that's like treating a pinched nerve with an aspirin. For the moment you feel relief. The throbbing subsides, but the underlying issue remains untreated. You've masked the pain at best. As time passes, your pinched nerve gets progressively worse—if not permanently mutilated. Now is the time to acknowledge the frayed state of your emotions and seek a proper solution.

Maybe you can identify with Stacey or Gail. Or perhaps you're a guy who has been hurt deeply by divorce. Rejection is already beginning to harden your heart. Sammy was such a guy. Sam's first wife walked out on him after six years of marriage. She suddenly announced that she decided to be a lesbian instead.

> **The temptation ... those who are now without a spouse face is to stop the leak in their emotional dam by plugging it with instant intimacy.**

Heavyweight boxing champion Mohammed Ali couldn't have hurled a harder punch to Sam's ego. We guys seem to be particularly sensitive when scorned by a woman we love. Far too many men never recover and spend much of their lives "getting back" at women rather than seeking healing.

How about you?

Do you want to successfully break the chains from the past? Would you like to avoid entering the bondage of false sexual intimacy in the future? Then prayerfully and constructively confront your situation. Put to use the principles we're about to examine and consider reviewing the following resources on reentering the single life. I've studied two very practical tools to help you get started on the right path: *Life After Divorce* by Bobbie Reed (Concordia) and *The Single-Again Handbook* by Thomas Jones (Nelson).

As you move toward becoming whole in Christ, as you restore your damaged self-esteem, you'll find sexual intimacy constantly ringing the doorbell to your heart. Excuses, rationalizations, and lies will work overtime to get you to compromise your commitment to celibacy. Don't invite that guest inside. In fact, examine with me three prominent deceptions which are sure to come calling.

Swimming with the Piranha

"Voraciously carnivorous."

My dictionary uses those two biting words to describe the piranha fish. It's not an exaggeration to suggest the same colorful language applies to the two-legged variety—the man or woman who attempts to draw you away from your stance on sexual purity. I might add that these deadly fish entice in two ways: by their casual willingness and easy availability, or by their directly applied pressure on your weakness.

In the sea of singleness, you'll find three varieties of piranha swimming at your side. They are: sex with an "ex"; sex with a sympathetic confidant; and sex with a predator. Let's catch these little carnivores and de-bone them one at a time.

Sex with an "Ex"

This may be the most obvious fish to spot, but it's a tough one to fry. Let's say you still see your former spouse socially. As time passes, it's easy to overlook the reason why the marriage bond was severed. You're tempted to fill the void inside by giving yourself to one another. After all, you're familiar with each other's bodies. You know what buttons to push. And it's possible your sexual expression bordered on awesome. It might have been the *one* thing you both agreed upon and did well together.

But sex with an "ex" won't fix a broken marriage.

Furthermore, it's wrong, unjustifiable, and incredibly destructive. That's the advice from Dr. Bobbie Reed. Even though she spent ten years as a single mom, Dr. Reed insists, "When the marriage relationship is dissolved, physical intimacy is no longer appropriate. It is just as wrong to have sex with your former spouse as it is to have sex with a new partner."[2]

> **Excuses, rationalizations, and lies will work over-time to get you to compromise your commitment to celibacy.**

Listen to the apostle Paul as he addresses sex outside of marriage: "Flee from sexual immorality. All other sins a man commits are outside his body, but he who sins sexually sins against his own body. Do you not know that your body is a temple of the Holy Spirit, who is in you, whom you have received from God? You are not your own; you were bought at a price. Therefore honor God with your body" (1 Cor. 6:18–20).

When Paul wrote these inspired words, I don't recall him tucking in an exclusion clause. He didn't say, "Oh, and for those who were once married, no problem if you feel the urge to indulge in sex with your ex." On the contrary, he said our bodies are not our own to do with as we please. We must "honor God" with our body. That applies to the single, the engaged, and the formerly married persons.

Besides, have we forgotten about the whole point of this book? Sexual intimacy draws two people together before the Lord who designed our frame. If the sexual expression doesn't please the Lord it won't satisfy beyond the moment. Sex with an "ex" may provide temporary relief to the loneliness you feel—but drugs could do the same thing. Both are out of bounds.

Sex with a Sympathetic Confidant

"We didn't mean to have sex," Joseph informed me. "Marci was just attempting to be a supportive friend after my wife died. One night she put her arm around me to comfort the hurt inside. It felt so good to be close to a woman again. Smelling her slight fragrance re-ignited those feelings I thought were gone forever." They engaged in sex for a season. As they did, the whole thing fell apart—their sexual intimacy was built on a shallow foundation.

> **If the sexual expression doesn't please the Lord, it won't satisfy beyond the moment.**

This variety of piranha is more difficult to detect. Why? Because they swim into your life offering a listening ear, a shoulder to cry on, and words of encouragement to help you stay afloat. I'd hazard a guess that few confidants come alongside of you with ulterior motives. I imagine Marci truly wanted to be a buddy to Joseph. But when a major tragedy like the loss of a spouse strikes, our emotional and spiritual defenses become drained. We're intensely vulnerable. If not extremely careful, we open the door to despair.

As wonderful as it might be to discover one who cares and supports you in your time of grief, fight the tendency to drift into sexual intimacy. Don't take the bait. It's not God's best no matter how nice it looks on the surface. If the temptation appears too strong, clutch onto these words of hope: "No temptation has seized you except what is common to man. And God is faithful; he will not let you be tempted beyond what you can bear. But when you are tempted, he will also provide a way out so that you can stand up under it" (1 Cor. 10:13).

Sex with a Predator

The last of the piranha I'd like to look at can be found just about anywhere. You can usually tell one because they don't mince words. Often, their approach resembles the pressure tactics you feel from a used car salesman. They interrogate you with questions like, "What do you have to lose? You're not a virgin anymore." Or, "You have physical needs so why not meet them?"

I'll give this piranha some credit: you *do* have physical drives—but sex with a predator is definitely the wrong way of satisfying them. If you ever find yourself dating one, keep in mind God would never want you to settle for someone who disrespects your commitment to Christ.

Respect yourself! Trust me, you can do much better.

The problem you face is often one of receiving the Lord's acceptance and forgiveness—especially following a divorce. Realize that God loves you. He accepts you just as you are. Can you accept that? If you buy the lie that he doesn't want you, you'll be tempted to run to the arms of another for intimate acceptance.

What About the Albino Crow?

All crows are black. I've witnessed big black crows basking in the sun on power lines, black crows ensconcing comfortably on a fence, or black crows soaring through the sky. But I have never observed a crow sporting a different color. Have you? Well then, they must all be black. We were having this argument in college. Can you guess which course? Yeah, philosophy.

In the heat of the debate my professor asked, "What about the albino crow?" Huh? Everybody knows albinos are creatures who suffer a loss of pigment. There are albino bunnies, cats, even human beings, but a crow? Yes, somewhere flying proudly across the terrain is a pure white crow.

The fact that they're rare—and I haven't seen one—doesn't alter the fact they exist.

Here's the parallel to our conversation.

When all you've known is hurt, pain, and brokenness, you may be deceived into concluding "that's just the way it is." When everyone around you uses sex to cope, you might reason that doing the same is your only hope. Since following God's design might seem futile, you attempt to fulfill your sexual intimacy desires apart from getting remarried.

Don't make that mistake.

For the divorcee, maybe you never witnessed a healthy marriage. Yours was a stormy mess at best. Perhaps the same was true of your parents' experience. And when friends confide things are rocky for them, it would be understandable (but incorrect) if you concluded that "marriage is for the birds."

> **When all you've known is hurt, pain, and brokenness, you may be deceived into concluding "that's just the way it is."**

In spite of what you might not have seen—like the albino crow—a significant percentage of marriages *are* vibrant. (My analogy breaks down because strong marriages, thankfully, are not as rare as an albino bird!) Accept the fact that the Lord may one day bless you with an awesome marriage—the only place to freely enjoy sex.

As a matter of fact, the view from my chair is radically different than what most see. My Greek lineage can be traced back five generations. If you were to study our family tree you'd find that there has been *only one divorce* in the entire clan! Without question, that's the Lord's doing. By contrast to your present position, do you see how easy it would be for me to assume that all marriages are strong?

Regardless of your vantage point, marriage was ordained by God. It's not a faulty design—the Manufacturer hasn't

issued a recall. There's no reason to trade in previous disap-
pointments for a trunk full of future regrets. Running past
remarriage and into the arms of uncommitted sexual intimacy is always a dance with disaster.

There's a better road to travel. Here are a few pointers
to help you go the distance:

1. Plug into a solid church.

You won't witness good marriages sitting at the local bar.
Nor will you receive godly guidance from the bartender.
And, it's safe to say, you'd be hard pressed to discover sound
marriages amidst the flashing lights and thundering music
on the dance floor at "Flirts" nightclub.
If you're ever to have a prayer of wit-
nessing a great marriage, get plugged
into a good church and study the solid
marriages you'll find there.

**You won't
witness good
marriages
sitting at the
local bar.**

In chapter 2 we discussed the importance of good role models. I challenged
you to learn how to be an awesome,
godly lover from those who are doing it right. Motivational
speaker and best-selling author Anthony Robbins agrees.
"Find a role model, someone who's already getting the
results you want," he counsels. "Learn what they're doing,
what their core beliefs are, and how they think."[3] Do you
want to be the best? Then study the best.

Want to recharge your spiritual batteries? Then go
where the gospel takes center stage. Doing so will provide
you with the fellowship we all so desperately need. In the
words of the apostle Paul, "Do not be yoked together with
unbelievers. For what do righteousness and wickedness have
in common? Or what fellowship can light have with darkness? What harmony is there between Christ and Belial?
What does a believer have in common with an unbeliever?"
(2 Cor. 6:14–15).

2. Rebuild your accountability and support network.

Whether single, married, widowed, or divorced, all of us can benefit from an accountability partner. I've discovered there are two primary types of people needed to completely satisfy this vital aspect of our discipleship. There's the individual who helps us stay on track with certain objectives we've set for ourselves. These goals include weight loss, breaking or forming habits, maintaining a regular prayer life, or sticking to an educational goal.

The second kind of accountability accomplice is a special friend. This partner can be called upon—anytime. He or she is someone you can call and say, "I'm about to do something stupid . . . *help*!" They're the type that you've given permission to get into your face—and stay there until you straighten up. Ask yourself, "Do I have these kind of supports backing me up?" If not, why not?

3. Dwell on what you have—not what you lack.

Look around you. Are you and/or your children healthy? Give thanks. Are you clothed, fed, and sufficiently housed? Give thanks. Do you have an income stream—however big or small? Give thanks. Do you possess control over the majority of your bodily functions? Rejoice! The next time you find your spirit sagging, speak words of thanks and praise—you'll be surprised what happens.

That's exactly what King David did throughout his life. In fact, if my math is correct, David uses the word *praise* 210 times in the Psalms. The next time you're tempted to sing the blues, consider a new song: "Why are you downcast, O my soul? Why so disturbed within me? Put your hope in God, for I will yet praise him, my Savior and my God" (Ps. 43:5).

4. Discover alternate sources for appropriate physical contact.

For me, this includes participation in sports, nieces and

nephews walking on my back and legs, and back massages by a guy friend (or by the specialist at the YMCA when I have an extra $15). I've also found that visiting a "huggy" family enables me to meet my "hug quota" on a regular basis. It's amazing how reassuring a "bear" hug can be. Kissing it ain't—but it sure beats feeling like you're sentenced to solitary confinement.

A number of friends have reported that pets offer warmth and love in a way that helps them retain their sanity. I've trained my parrots to say "I love you" ... now if only I could get them to say, "You're the best!"

Opportunity Is Knocking

As we've discussed, far too many single-again adults reach for sexual intimacy to fill the void they feel inside. Remember Gail's letter? She attempted to fill her emptiness inappropriately. Instead of guiding her energies in a productive and rewarding direction, she reached for the forbidden fruit of passing pleasure. The bitter aftertaste was hard to swallow.

Let me ask you several questions.

If you could do *anything* in the world, what would you do? What dreams have you suppressed after the loss of your spouse? Which talents have you put into semi-retirement? What special skills have you traded-in for temporary sexual intimacy? As you consider your answers, don't dare give me the "I'm no big deal" routine. And don't berate yourself with thoughts like: "What do I have to offer, anyway?" or "Who cares what my dreams are?"

That line of thinking is pure, unadulterated hogwash.

You disagree? Better reread the parable of the ten talents in Matthew 25:14–29. Jesus makes it clear you and I have been assigned at least one—if not several—unique talents to invest. Why? He trusts in your ability to put them to good use. Did that register? Your heavenly Father believes in and places full confidence in you—even if you're widowed or divorced. He longs for you to make the most of your God-given abilities because it would bring him (and you) great joy!

> **Your heavenly Father believes in and places full confidence in you—even if you're widowed or divorced.**

This is why I feel it necessary to remind you that Jesus calls you to live *today*—not a year from now and not a year ago! Which means, of course, you'll need to fight the tendency to withdraw from the human race. As the saying goes, "the turtle only makes progress when he sticks his neck out." The opportunities that await you will require the same fortitude as our reptile friend.

The good news is you don't have to do it alone. Take to heart these encouraging words from Isaiah: "Those who hope in the LORD will renew their strength. They will soar on wings like eagles; they will run and not grow weary, they will walk and not be faint" (Isa. 40:31). That promise applies even to those who are single again.

Simply put, seize the moment. He'll supply the strength.

Go ahead, unlock your dreams. Reenter the land of the living. Lean on the Lord and take a risk. Do something you've always wanted to do. This is the start of a fresh chapter in your life. Have fun filling in the pages.

Why not volunteer to visit the elderly once a week—Sunday afternoons are perfect. Too afraid to leave the security of familiar surroundings? No problem. Let fresh opportunities come to you. Open your home and try your hand at leading a small group Bible study. How about teaching a Sunday school class for youngsters?

The key is to start somewhere, anywhere.

I recall the first time I visited a retirement home. I was in ninth grade—complete with shoulder-length hair and pimples on my face! Most middle school students aren't known to possess strong self-confidence. That's probably why my teacher suggested we reach out to those who might not otherwise have a visitor. He figured we'd gain confidence by giving of ourselves—and he was right!

Jesus calls you to live today—not a year from now.

Without exception, we were received with open arms. I still have to laugh. Because of my long hair, several dear souls thought I was with the Girl Scouts! I still remember Elizabeth. Liz and I hit it off, and even several years into college I'd return for a warm, rewarding chat. She's been dead for some time, but the delight she brought me is hard to forget.

You can do the same by giving yourself permission to build new memories. As you venture forward, you'll make new friends. You'll begin to see yourself in new ways. Your confidence will grow as you discover that you really do have a contribution to make. More importantly, you'll be less tempted to play sexual conquest games in order to rebuild your sense of worth.

As you capture these moments and put them to kingdom use, something else will happen. You'll buy yourself *time*—time to rebuild the right foundation for future expressions of intimacy. Why is this so important? Because sexual intimacy and remarriage—though understandably desirable—should not be your primary goal. Instead,

1. fix your eyes on becoming whole in Christ, and
2. use your unique talents to advance his kingdom.

With these aspirations as your primary focus, you'll pacify far more than a passing urge for physical attention; you'll satisfy the hunger that resides within your soul.

PART TWO

Preparing for Dynamic Sex and Satisfying Intimacy

CHAPTER 5

The Single Cycle

There's a girl, my Lord, in a flatbed Ford,
slowing down to take a look at me.
—*The Eagles*

Two are better than one because they have a
good return for their labor.
—*Ecclesiastes 4:9 NAS*

*Y*ou would almost have to see it to believe it.

The aging Volkswagen Rabbit was parked in a spot nobody could possibly miss in downtown Reno, Nevada. With white poster boards taped on several sides, the car conveyed an urgent message to those who passed by. In bold type Randy, the owner of this eyesore-on-wheels, hand-printed the message: WIFE WANTED.

Complete with a phone number, this desperate soul pleaded, "Make me happy! Please don't be afraid to talk to me." He actually included a photocopy of his paycheck, explaining "I would like to provide for you. I will work and pay rent." He assured potential candidates this offer was "not a joke." As if it would help, his photograph—which resembled a picture taken from a police line-up—was affixed to the side and rear car window.

For those who didn't immediately gravitate to becoming his life-long helpmate, Randy proposed, "I would like to get to know you . . . Consiter [sic] any offer." What if the long distance phone call was too costly for some? No problem. Just dial "collect." Oh, anytime day or night would be 81 convenient. His phone number was described as a "24-hour hot line."

Some people will do *anything* to find a mate.

After the smile faded from my face, I reflected that in some ways I was no different than Randy. I may never have been driven in a fit of desperation to plaster signs on my car soliciting a would-be wife. But like this man I've never met, I feel the intense longing to discover that special someone to spend my life with. I imagine you've been there, too.

Which should come as no surprise.

Deep within every single is a God-given desire for healthy intimacy. A hand to hold. Not to mention dynamic sex, children, and someone with whom to share the chapters of our life. During moments of total honesty, I've had to admit to myself that I frequently vacillate across a wide range of emotions. At one end of the spectrum, I'm completely contented. On the other, I feel cheated because— for whatever reason—it seems that *God* has withheld something good from me.

My hunch is you may have had similar feelings.

It's worth pointing out that a number of very distinct steps connect these two extremes. The Single Cycle starts here. This chapter will identify the six stages of the emotional cycle virtually all singles experience: contentment, restlessness, depression, poor choices, intense guilt, and a return to contentment.

Interestingly, as you'll soon see, I've discovered my sexuality as a single adult is intensely impacted by the various stages of the cycle.

Learning to "short-circuit" the negative aspects of the cycle—with its impact on our understanding of sex and intimacy—will be one of the benefits of our study together. You see, happily there *is* a healthy way to navigate the single cycle. Additionally, the balance of the book will provide a practical strategy to help you prepare yourself to experience deep intimacy now—and dynamic sex at such time that the Lord provides you with a spouse.

Friday Follies

It's Friday evening and the weekend is finally here. Come to think of it, the last few days were actually brimming with satisfying opportunities for ministry. For the moment, I feel contented—at peace, thank you. I don't mind that I'm single and that my hormones still must wait to discover the mystery of the marriage bed. Nor does it matter that my house is devoid of "homey" sounds generated by a wife, children, and their activity.

The silence is a welcome friend.

Presently, I feel comfortable with the understanding of the foundational principle of this book: marriage and sex should not be my objective—rather, becoming a godly lover is my goal. I'm even okay with the fact that most of my peers are committed to the opposite agenda, as they launch their weekly one-night stand ritual. No thanks, not for me. I'm different.

I've always been different—even as teenager. Oh, I looked the same in many ways—shoulder-length hair, tattered army jacket, and a '68 Dodge with air shocks jacked up in the back. But while my friends were getting high, racing cars, having sex—and getting secret abortions, I was radically involved in the Jesus People movement. We'd stuff "underground" Jesus newspapers in lockers around school and witness at the bowling alley, a favorite teen hang-out.

Way back then, my parents helped me to practice embracing the words of Jesus in Matthew 6:33, "But seek first his kingdom and his righteousness, and all these things will be given to you as well." In other words, the primary purpose of my life is to use it to advance the kingdom in whatever way the Lord had in mind.

That's why I feel so comfortable with my singleness—today.

Not surprisingly, I learned following the advice of this passage is one of the best ways to utilize my energies as a single male. The apostle Paul was absolutely on target when he observed, "One who is unmarried is concerned about the things of the Lord, how he may please the Lord; but one who is married is concerned about the things of the world, how he may please his wife, and his interests are divided" (1 Cor. 7:32–34 NAS).

If you've ever put in those extra hours lending a hand at the soup pantry, assisting the crisis pregnancy center, or stopping to change a tire for a stranded motorist, you know what I'm saying. It's a wonderful feeling to have the *freedom* to enrich the lives of those around you—in a planned way, or upon impulse. As a single, my time and money can be generously directed to advance the work of the Lord—truly a place of contentment.

However, I'm amazed how often it's the *little* things that can trigger feelings of discontentment in my spirit, that can rattle me out of this peaceful frame of mind. Take, for instance, the answering machine.

I'm amazed how often it's the little things that can trigger feelings of discontentment.

Has this ever happened to you? Throwing the keys on the counter, I check the number of messages received on my answering machine. The bright digital display glares back at me with the sum total of . . . ZERO. After determining my phone service *is* still functioning, I have to come to terms with the reality that *nobody* has called—again.

"It's another Friday night and I ain't got nobody"—a line from an old song—drifts through the silence of my life. Ahh. I don't believe I'm asking for much. It just would be nice to be assured someone cared that I existed. Thanks to that ridiculous machine, I find myself beginning to grow unsettled with my lot in life—an indication that stage two of the cycle (restlessness) is around the corner.

Maybe it's not the Code-A-Phone that triggered a change in your emotional state. It might be something as innocuous as the fortune cookie at the end of a quiet dinner. The other day, mine promised, "Your love life will be happy and harmonious." Yeah, right. A nice thought. "So why am I eating alone?" I reflected as I paid the bill.

Just that quickly, the seeds of discontentment were planted. Funny—it seems driving home I began to notice couples walking hand-in-hand or playing in the park. I'm glad for them, but ... for the first time in a while I wonder, *What about* me? I get irritable at the plain fact I'm alone, while it seems the rest of the world is having fun, experiencing intimacy, and enjoying the gift of sex.

In our fallen world, I would concede the second stage in the Single Cycle is virtually inevitable. That fact doesn't make it any easier to swallow. However, the way in which you and I respond to the Friday Follies is actually a sign of Christian maturity. Further, our response to it, as you'll see momentarily, is also the key to maintaining or breaking the Single Cycle.

Sleepless in Seattle

In 1993, moviegoers were charmed by the romantic comedy, *Sleepless in Seattle*. Hearts throbbed and tears flowed freely as audiences related to Tom Hanks' character, Sam Baldwin. At the outset, we learn Sam is a single parent immersed in feelings of loneliness and sadness, due to the loss of his wife to cancer. His friends offer little comfort.

Trying to alleviate his father's pain, Sam's son, Jonah, dials a late night talk show for advice. Through a series of events, Sam's mailbox is jammed with letters from prospective dates—including one from investigative reporter Annie Reed (Meg Ryan). The "power of love" almost mystically draws Annie to Sam. Ah, true love.

The music swelled, the credits rolled, and couples left the theater hugging one another just a bit closer. Personally, I found myself identifying with a number of the emotions contributing to Sam's sleeplessness. The awkwardness of dating in a world of "aggressive females," mustering the will to date someone new, and feeling the odds are not in my favor that something might *actually* work out. I can understand why Sam initially retreated from the human race.

The absence of social activity—specifically of a date—over time leads to the third stage of the Single Cycle: depression. At the heart of this stage is self-pity. You might call it the "woe is me" syndrome. If honest, you and I arrive at the alarming conclusion that *God* is actually our problem. After all, he could say the word, and I wouldn't be sleeping alone anymore.

At times, this depression is difficult to hide.

Noticing that the bounce in my step has been replaced by a slow shuffle, my married friends attempt to provide their analysis of my situation. "But, Bob," they interject, "perhaps God has kept you single in order that you can do more kingdom work." That sounds fair. You get to share the carnival of joys that spousal companionship brings and, perhaps, a family—while I get to work. Hmm. My skin starts to crawl with resentment.

> If honest, you and I arrive at the alarming conclusion that God is actually our problem.

In the face of comments by these modern-day advisors to Job, I'm still married to the dream set forth in Genesis. One man. One woman. Brought together by God. Designed for each other. Commissioned for the purpose of being fruitful. I like fruit—especially those that could one day look me in the eye and say, "I love you, Daddy."

I once asked an associate, "How do you feel when someone provides that counsel—that we're kept single to advance the kingdom?"

She responded, "I'd like to slap their smug little faces!" Then she added, thoughtfully, "It may be true, but I don't need *married* people giving me that advice."

You see, at the heart of the third stage of the Single Cycle lies what could be called "the death of a dream."

That one phrase aptly describes what virtually every single I've spoken with feels as he or she drifts into adulthood—alone and hungry for intimacy. Digging around the smoldering ashes, I find that most of us are not single by choice. Rather, a surprising number, if truthful, would confess that *their* script called for true love at age twenty-one, marriage by twenty-three, and a start on children by twenty-six. The car, house with a white picket fence, and a career path all neatly carved out by thirty.

Yet things didn't work out that way. Alone and very single, this dream of marital union is beginning to look more like an inexplicable nightmare. As a thirty-seven-year-old single I should know. If you're reading this, chances are that your desire to be married remains unfulfilled too.

For some women, maybe part of the glorified plans for the perfect companion can be traced back to Barbie's Dream House and Car. I can't say for sure. One way or another, at a very young age the seeds of our fantasy family—not to mention a timetable for it to happen—were sown. What *is* certain is that things haven't worked out the way we singles had expected. The dating game is just that, a game. A cruel one at best. For whatever reason, a lifetime love remains outside of our grasp.

Maybe your story was different. You had a wonderful, near picture-perfect marriage. Then, one day, the news of your spouse's death rocked your world. Or maybe it wasn't

The dating game is just that, a game. A cruel one at best. For whatever reason, a lifetime love remains outside of our grasp.

death that stole your love, but the arms of another. Betrayed by death or adultery, in either case you're left alone holding the bag. That's why the depression in stage three can be so very intense.

In our depressed state, we begin to wonder if there is actually something wrong with us—"Am I that unattractive?" It's even likely that we might wonder, "Is God mad at me?"

You see, what's especially puzzling is that the Lord appears to ignore our healthy, God-honoring desire to please him with a Christian home. So if God is standing in the way, guess what? Taking charge of our own destiny appears to be the only option. Here's where many Christian singles contemplate poor choices—the makings of the fourth stage of the Single Cycle.

PEANUTS reprinted by permission of United Feature Syndicate, Inc.

Reach Out and Touch Someone?

Working our way around the cycle, we've moved from contentment, to restlessness, into depression, and now stand on the threshold of stage four: poor choices.

Enough of this seeking the kingdom stuff. It hasn't worked. "In fact," at this stage the single may reflect, "my mirror informed me this morning I now have gray hair in places that hair ought not be growing. My patience runneth out. Seems I'm just going to take matters into my own hands." Stage four is perhaps the most dangerous and potentially explosive aspect of the Single Cycle. Why? Because taking matters into our own hands is *always* hazardous.

For many, our God-given sex drive further exacerbates this stage of the cycle. Speaking of sex drive, author Jerry Jenkins describes men as "equipped with an engine that idles like a rocket, but which isn't supposed to be launched for years."[1] At thirty-seven, I can relate! After all, I'm a warm-blooded Greek. Naturally, I've wondered why God placed fiery hormones in my body that woke up when I was twelve, but have been in a "holding pattern" for more than twenty years!

> Why did God place fiery hormones in my body that woke up when I was twelve, but have been in a "holding pattern" for more than twenty years?

Certainly women have a parallel longing for intimacy. However described, men and women alike find their lack of an appropriate sexual expression complicating the feelings of depression. Why, my hormones informed me the other day that unless they see some action soon, they'll find a different body!

Based upon responses to my informal singles survey, I know I'm not the only one who is dealing with sexuality in light of the Singles Cycle. I asked participants how they deal with the depression described in the previous stage. See if their responses ring a bell with you.

Take Amy. Her twenty-eighth birthday party provided an annoying reminder: one of her lifelong wishes didn't come true since she last blew out these candles. Still single, Amy moved through the first three stages—contentment, restlessness, depression—and now admits she's ready to entertain the unthinkable.

In her case, she opted to throw herself into a short-term relationship with someone—*anyone*. It mattered not whether it was a healthy arrangement. It might even be with an "ex," someone she *knows* is not good for her. Amy's bottom line went something like this: anybody *has* to be better than nobody. A sexual liaison ensued.

Allen, a thirty-three-year-old professional, inhaled large doses of unhealthy food—overeating was his poison. Sally spent money she didn't have on excessive shopping to bolster her sagging spirit and need for attention. Karen darkened the doors of a dance club with one purpose: to get noticed. (Unfortunately, given her already low self-esteem, she was the perfect candidate for a smooth talker with a one-night stand on his mind.) Dave dabbled in the wretched world of pornography. Brent used alcohol to numb his feelings of depression.

Betty withdrew from friends and family. Steve copped a highly critical attitude about his friends who had a girlfriend or boyfriend. Rebellious rock music provided a release for Robert. Mary surrounded herself with activity so she didn't have to deal with her depressed heart.

What about you? When stage four knocks on your door, what poor choices might you be tempted to make?

The Pathway of Regret

Admittedly, these are slow, lonely miles to walk on the road of life. It's a most tiring route. And talk about a barren,

God-forsaken landscape. The view of life from an empty sofa in a single person's apartment can be, well, bleak at best. The terrain looks a lot like how we singles sometimes feel—forgotten by God. For some, the death of their dream leads to a state of personal panic. It's where we entertain the unthinkable choices discussed in the previous section.

For me, those poor choices included resuscitating a relationship with Vicki that I knew was a dead end. When my companions got wind of my renewed contact with her, they quickly reminded me I was pursuing a friendship that was bad news. But given the depression I was experiencing at the time, I rationalized that there wasn't any real harm in reopening this closed chapter. Boy, did I figure wrong.

You see, Vicki never experienced love and acceptance from her father. As a result, she found it difficult to receive and enjoy love from another male. No matter how many books we read together about the pain she had internalized, no matter how much affirmation and support I offered, Vicki remained a prisoner of the past. In fact, I had previously spent five years of my life determined to smooth out her turbulence—but to no avail. I'll be the first to admit returning to a failed relationship is an easy trap to fall into—a temptation that must be resisted at all cost.

Stage five, intense guilt, follows participation in poor choices. You can be sure that anyone who allowed panic and desperation to tempt them to settle for anyone or anything as a solution to their depression will experience a day of reckoning. They'll come to their senses and realize the dumb decision for what it was, dumb.

No, something isn't always better than nothing. If you don't believe me that an individual can be motivated to drastic measures, you're either not single, or you haven't observed the personal section of the newspaper lately. One particular appeal says it all. Brace yourself. What you're about to read is a bona fide ad from a San Francisco daily.

Wanted: Girlfriend. Single or married. Good-looking, sexy, intelligent companion between thirty and forty. Must be extremely flexible and undemanding. Willing to tryst approximately one night a week (for at least two hours, preferably at your house). Prefer to stay in and have dinner cooked (will provide occasional bottle of wine) since going out in public presents risks. Possibility of one or two overnight weekends a year, if convenient for me and you are available, discreet, and willing to pay your own way.

But wait, it gets worse . . .

Must be a good listener, have a strong sex drive and be aggressive, but not pushy. Willing to wait for convenient time to hear from me about time and place to get together. Must not try to contact me by phone. Too risky.

What's this self-centered fella's bottom line? Read on.

Possibility for long-term relationship, if you can wait it out until my kids are out of high school—unless I meet someone who is less demanding or more accessible.

Married But Needing More[2]

As hard as it is to believe, this personal ad—according to Ann Landers who reprinted this bizarre personal—actually attracted a number of responses to his selfish appeal for adulterous affection. Talk about desperate!

The longer I remain single, the more I can empathize with the individual who feels driven to responding to such an ad. Admittedly that sounds very unspiritual at first glance. But that's the painful reality. You see, we singles start to believe that if God were fair, he'd pass out a sheet of paper with everyone's name listed on it. Inscribed beside our name would be the name of the perfect mate—complete with phone number and address.

This, no doubt, would be a much simpler process than

the current system of meeting new people. You know, dreaming up creative dates, spending money you don't have, making small talk, paying large phone bills ... in many cases ending up with nothing more than dashed expectations and, more often than not, a broken heart.

You'd think we singles would qualify for combat pay.

Yes, as an alternative, a printout from God would be simpler—but definitely boring. So the manual search for a mate continues—one day, one date at a time. Sometimes with rather exhausting results. That is why we can fall into a state of loneliness and depression, followed by the inappropriate choices. Guilt comes to us at night and, with its satanic fumes, smothers us in the mistakes we've made.

When confronted by our feelings of guilt, we singles may start to believe that God must be angry with us and forgiveness may not be possible. This can happen even if we didn't actually compromise our moral principles. For me, the fact that I may have come *close* is scary enough.

One of Satan's greatest tricks is to haunt the Christian single who made a bad choice—or who is habitually making poor choices. Some spin their wheels in their guilt for many weeks, even months. One sign of Christian maturity in the single is when he can readily come to terms with his decision, accept the responsibility, ask for forgiveness, and move back into a right relationship with his first Love, Jesus Christ.

> One sign of Christian maturity in the single is when he can readily come to terms with his decision, accept the responsibility, and ask for forgiveness.

When Peace Like a River

We've now gone full circle in the Single Cycle. Happily, a breath of fresh air can flow once again through the heart of a single from the Savior, reassuring him or her that he is very much in charge. The final stage is a return to those rich feelings of contentment described in the first place.

Personally speaking, the process leading me to this place of renewed and relatively long spans of peace was through much soul searching after a failed romance, and a few words of wisdom written by C. H. Spurgeon. Allow me to explain.

Her name was Sandy. It was spring and love was in the air. I first met her in the company cafeteria—talk about electric! Our chemistry (whatever that means) immediately clicked. Both of us found each other irresistible. For the first time in many years I believed I found someone who I'd truly enjoy spending my life with. All of our friends validated the relationship, and we were moving very seriously toward the direction of marriage.

Without boring you with the gory details, much to everyone's surprise, we broke up and she married another. I was devastated—mad at God is more like it. Why in the world would God apparently grant me the desire of my heart, only to withdraw it just as the relationship was ripening on the vine? This playful, fun-loving, beautiful, and talented woman evaporated before my eyes. In an instant, I was thrust into a deep depression.

After several weeks of spinning my wheels in the mire of self-pity, I found myself reading a devotional by C. H. Spurgeon. That particular evening, he asked a number of pointed questions pertaining to our confidence in Christ. He asked, "Are you anxious about temporal things this evening? You trust in Jesus for your salvation. Then why are you troubled?" In other words, I freely confess that I trust God for my *eternal* affairs, so why am I not trusting him for earthly matters of importance to me, too?

Score two points for the good doctor.

Spurgeon—with the skill of a surgeon—cut deep with his next observation. "Is God enough for your need, or is his all-sufficiency too narrow for you? Is his heart faint? Is his arm weary? If so, seek another God."[3] Wow! I felt like Spurgeon whacked me across my rump with a giant two-by-four. Of course there are no other gods to seek. So focused on what I *didn't* have, I began to doubt the Lord was who he said he is.

> So focused on what I didn't have, I began to doubt the Lord was who he said he is.

Through this experience I learned that the Lord still had the perfect plan for my life—and that includes the details pertaining to a spouse, as well as my sexuality. After all, God hasn't made a mistake yet. I may not be able to comprehend his ways, but his track record is much better than mine. Yes, Jesus *can* be trusted.

Short-circuiting the Cycle

I once detailed the six stages of the cycle for a female coworker, and I'll never forget her comment. Becky observed, "Be sure to indicate that we singles can experience these six steps all in the *same* day!" She's right.

For some, the morning light finds them perfectly comfortable with their singleness. But by late morning someone or something triggers the mild restlessness of spirit. Eating lunch alone, depression can squeeze its troublesome foot in the door of the heart. Leaving work, unchecked feelings may lead to a poor choice to pacify the pain. Bugged by a guilty conscience, evening devotions pave the way for a return to trust in God.

Becky's observation is insightful. At the same time, there are others who linger in any one stage of the Single Cycle for days, weeks—even longer. So how do you and I break the vicious voyage? Several ideas come to mind which, I might add, I've had two decades to field test!

1. Be thankful for your singleness.

As a teenager (back before videotape was invented), I

listened with interest to a hit song on the radio in which the singer lamented being alone. I believe the title was "One Is the Loneliest Number." Listening to this depressing ditty you'd think only couples had a life!

Excuse me, but being single isn't a deadly disease. Singleness isn't a form of punishment by an angry God. It actually has numerous benefits. As hard as it may seem to do on the surface, *thanking* the Lord "in all things" helps you and me to cultivate and maintain a spirit of contentment.

2. Work on who you are becoming, not what you have.

Larry Crabb has observed that God doesn't *owe* us a marriage partner. And that *no* relationship will ever be enough on this side of heaven. With that in mind, wisdom would suggest that you and I need to concentrate on nurturing our spirit. When we're focused on *becoming* the best possible mate—rather than expending a significant portion of our energy trying to catch one—we'll be in a better position not to be sucked into the Single Cycle.

3. Cultivate nonsexual expressions of intimacy.

If a Martian were to come to America today and accidentally land in front of a television set, he'd develop a distorted view of human behavior. Among other things, he'd be led to think that all intimate contact is sexual. And if he spent an afternoon filling his Martian brain with images from MTV, he'd assume virtually everyone is engaged in mass quantities of sexual contact.

Not surprisingly, many of us hold to the same mistaken perspective. Part of breaking the cycle is learning to satisfy our need for intimacy in nonsexual ways. (See chapter 7 for a host of great ideas.)

4. Watch what you watch.

In my survey of singles, I asked for responders to identify things that might spark feelings of unhappiness as a single adult. (Remember, trigger mechanisms can easily propel us headlong into the cycle.) Interestingly, approximately seventy-five percent designated films, music, or romance novels as a primary culprit. One woman responded, "I thought the movie *Pretty Woman* was an exercise in masochism for single women—it was one more Cinderella fantasy to screw up our view of reality."

Personally, I've made a commitment to myself to be very selective about the things I read, watch, and listen to for personal recreation. Actually, it's a cue from King David, who cautions: "I will set no worthless thing before my eyes" (Ps. 101:3 NAS). That means eliminating salacious story lines, sexual situations, and sappy romantic drivel. Doing so helps me keep focused on who I'm becoming, rather than being reminded of what I lack.

True Love Waits

Navigating the negative stages of our emotional cycle is important. But what are we supposed to do with our hormones in the meanwhile? As promised, in the following pages I'll provide a sensible strategy to help us handle those stormy rascals.

Just do us both a favor. Don't go watching a sappy love story on television until we talk again!

CHAPTER 6

How to Handle Those Hormones

Sinners are much more fun, and only the good
die young.

—*Billy Joel, "Only the Good Die Young"*

For some people, sex becomes all they have to
live for, and naturally it becomes a big disap-
pointment.

—*Dr. Archibald Hart[1]*

*D*ay after day she followed his every movement
with longing eyes. In her mind this man was
the walking embodiment of youthful desire.
His body was so firm, so defined—so desirable. Her craving
for his physical attention drove her to the brink of insanity.
Regardless of the approach she used to seduce him, he
remained outside of her grasp.

His amazing resistance to her forward suggestions only
served to strengthen her resolve. She wanted him in the
worst way. Driven by the unwritten principle—we want
what we cannot have—she worked even harder to claim the
object of her lust. At night she lay awake wondering how
long he could resist. Yes, she was a married woman. But the
practice of adultery was common. Certainly that wasn't his
problem.

Her sleeplessness only produced more questions. Didn't
he have strong sexual urges, too? Don't young men feel a

burning desire for sexual fulfillment? A man his age should be at the height of his sexual prime—why doesn't he respond to her enticing advances? What makes him so strong?

Today would be different—they'd be alone. With the anticipation and confidence of a hunter she laid her trap. When he walked into the room, she'd drape herself across the soft, inviting sofa. Her painted eyes, the carefully selected satin clothes—even her perfume—were designed to be intentionally intoxicating. No man, she thought, would be able to think clearly at a moment like this.

Before she knew it, the time had come. There he stood, handsome in form and appearance. Her adulterous lips whispered only three poisonous words: "Lie with me!"

A Case of the "Flees"

Sounds like the action from a saucy romance novel, doesn't it? No, it's not a new fiction work by Danielle Steel. It's the biblical story of Potiphar's wife making a move on one fine-looking Hebrew youth by the name of Joseph. Go ahead and read the original version in Genesis 39 for yourself. You'll see how passionately this woman wanted Joseph's body.

What was Joseph's response to her sultry overtures? We're told "he left his garment in her hand, and fled" (v. 12 KJV). A healthy case of the "flees" energized his weak knees. Never mind diplomacy. Forget the jacket. There was no looking back.

Think about it. Joseph—who some biblical scholars place in his late teens—should have been flattered. This aristocrat was most likely a classy lady. Wealth afforded her Egypt's finest. And Joseph certainly didn't misread the meaning of her intentions: "Lie with me." Nothing ambiguous about that. If later interrogated, he could hardly be charged with sexual harassment.

Although the names of the participants have changed, in one form or another the same thing happens today. The call of an unfaithful spouse. The longing of a lonely lovesick date. Whatever the case, you and I know sexual temptation is a fact of life. We can either yield to its alluring invitation or muster the willpower to slip from its lustful grip.

What kept Joseph's hormones in check? Furthermore, what can we learn from his example? How *do* we throttle the fiery sex drive that rages within us? Those questions (among others) will be the springboard for our discussion in this chapter.

Pillow Talk

Billy Crystal has to be one of the funniest actors in the business. My side still aches from his routine as Mitch Robbins in *City Slickers*. This man, who's suffering a midlife crisis, tries to find meaning in his pitiful existence. At age forty he's lost his zip, and his smile has been long gone. To reenergize things, friends Phil Barquist (Daniel Stern) and Ed Furillo (Bruno Kirby) take him on a summer round-up.

Throughout their ride on the range, Ed—the Italian Stallion—constantly has sex and women on the brain. From his perspective, Mitch could use a fling to spice things up. But in one of those rare Hollywood moments, Mitch adamantly prefers fidelity. Frustrated, Ed pitches Mitch this improbable scenario to see if he would consider a tryst under the conditions of *total* secrecy.

You'll love Mitch's bottom line:

Ed: Let me ask you this: What if you could have sex with someone very attractive and Barbara [Mitch's wife] would never find out?

Mitch: It's a big trap. Look what happened to Phil. . . .

Ed: Yeah. Let's say a *spaceship* lands and the most beautiful

woman you ever saw gets out and all she wants to do is
have the greatest sex in the universe with you.

Mitch: Could happen.

Ed: And the second it's over, she flies away for eternity. No
one will *ever* know. You're telling me you wouldn't do
it?!

Mitch: No, because what you're describing actually happened to my cousin Ronald and his wife *did* find out
about it. They know *everything*.

Ed: Forget it....

Mitch: Look, Ed, what I'm saying—it wouldn't make it all
right if Barbara didn't know. *I'd* know and I wouldn't
like myself. That's all.

Perhaps there *is* hope for Hollywood!

Did you catch it? The issue for Mitch wasn't whether
or not such an affair would be discovered by the woman to
whom he pledged faithfulness—although that was important. The fact is, *he* would forever have the memories of
compromise haunting the recesses of his mind. For once
personal integrity won out over passing infidelity! Bravo!

When Potiphar's wife requested the presence of Joseph's
body in her bed, his personal integrity was on the line, too.
But it was something greater that kept Joseph's libido in
check. Listen to how he handled her overtures:

> With me around, my master does not concern himself
> with anything in the house, and he has put all that he
> owns in my charge. There is no one greater in this house
> than I, and he has withheld nothing from me except you,
> because you are his wife. How then could I do this great
> evil, and sin against God? (Gen. 39:8–9 NAS)

Isn't it interesting that this young Hebrew servant saw
adultery as an affront to God? It was this earnest desire to
honor God in all things that gave him the inner strength to

slap her adulterous option across the face. Let's be real about this. Don't entertain the thought that Joseph was some kind of Super-saint who could leap tall temptations with a single bound. He was wired exactly the same way you and I are . . . with perhaps one difference.

A plan.

The Next Thing You're Smoking Cigarettes

Listening to my buddies confess their moral failures over the years, I've observed a common thread. Harry made it clear that he never *meant* to have sexual intercourse with his date—it "just happened," he assured me. Frank used the same expression to describe his impromptu indiscretion. Andrea was beside herself: "I swear we didn't mean to go all the way, it just happened."

Since this problem appears to be so widespread, I've decided to coin a new term for the condition. You might call it the next-thing-I-knew-we-were-smoking-cigarettes syndrome. Say what?

I'm referring to the torrid love scenes on television. You know the ones—two people meet and talk about the stock market, but they find their mutual sexual urges hard to contain.

Blazing into action without any prior thought, they've ripped each other's clothing off. Presto! Before you know it, the participants are in bed smoking.

It "just happened."

> It was this earnest desire—to honor God in all things—that gave him the inner strength to slap her adulterous option across the face.

I don't buy it. With the exception of date rape, premarital sex doesn't "just happen" to anyone. Take Andrea's case. As she elaborated on her situation, I was surprised that she didn't recognize the number of *individual steps* she had climbed along the way. I counted twelve. Here's a brief outline of them:

1. Andrea accepted the invitation for a date with someone she knew had a questionable reputation. This guy was known for his sexual advances.

2. She agreed to have him prepare the meal at her place instead of insisting on a public restaurant.

3. She built a romantic fire to set the mood.

4. After dinner, they sat closely on the sofa to watch a video together.

5. They began adjusting the pillows and position and found it was more comfortable to snuggle on the floor facing the TV.

6. It got hot by the fire, so Andrea partially unbuttoned her blouse—at his suggestion.

7. There's nothing like having one's hair brushed so she willingly accepted his offer.

8. While the credits were rolling, she started to do a little rolling of her own—with him.

9. Exchanging back and shoulder massages is always easier without the hassle of a shirt.

10. The touch turned intimate.

11. The fire was lit in more places than just the hearth.

12. Andrea decided to respond to the moment and had sex.

Andrea could have avoided the next-thing-I-knew-we-were-smoking-cigarettes syndrome if, like Joseph, she had a plan. What was the formula that fueled his fortitude? Reviewing Joseph's sharp style, I picked up five distinct ingredients: know your bottom line, communicate your position, stick by your convictions, avoid compromising circumstances, and bolt like a bat.

Let's review these trade secrets individually.

1. Know your bottom line.

For Joseph, there was never really a question about the whole affair. Listen to his heart: "How then could I do this great evil, and sin against God?" Joseph understood the true nature of adulterous sex. Such behavior was:

1. A great evil and
2. A sin against God.

That, my friend, was his bottom line. A clear-cut, black and white standard. Entertaining her proposition was unthinkable. There could be no compromise.

Have you defined your bottom line? What's it based upon?

2. Communicate your position.

Determine that your stance on premarital sex is vital and communicate it to those around you. Doing so helps to place a protective hedge around you. Granted, there will be those who will attempt to penetrate this barrier—just watch what happened to Joseph:

> And it came about after these events that his master's wife looked with desire at Joseph, and she said, "Lie with me." (v. 7 NAS)

There she goes again, pounding on the boundaries. In verses eight and nine we're told that Joseph reinforced his position. He was reasonable, to the point, and perfectly clear. Sex with her was not a remote possibility—she didn't even have to read his mind because he spelled it out for her.

How about you?

3. Stick by your convictions.

It's amazing how this gal wouldn't take Joseph's "no" for an answer. Just watch her hammer away at his resolve:

> And it came about as she spoke to Joseph *day after day*,
> that he did not listen to her to lie beside her, or be with
> her. (v. 10 NAS, emphasis added)

In spite of her persistent pleas, Joseph stood his ground.
Which, when you consider she was probably as enticing as
any one of the *Sports Illustrated* swimsuit models, was an
amazing feat. You'll notice that he didn't even give an inch.
Not only did he reject the idea of sex with her, he wouldn't
"be with her." Long, quiet walks in the garden—forget it!
How about a cold drink over on the couch? Not an option.
Joseph gets high marks for sticking by his convictions. As I
mentioned previously, his personal integrity was far too
valuable.

Does your integrity have a price?

4. Avoid compromising circumstances.

We're told that Potiphar placed Joseph in charge of running his entire home. Evidently, Potiphar was a successful
business man who had little time for such details. Supervis-
ing his holdings in the field dominated Potiphar's energies.
Working *inside* of Potiphar's home was Joseph's job. No
compromise there.

In fact, if we can glean anything from his behavior it
wouldn't surprise me to learn that he always had several
assistants around him for accountability. But notice what
took place that fateful day:

> Now it happened one day that he went into the house to
> do his work, and none of the men of the household was
> there inside. (v. 11 NAS)

S-u-r-*prise!* No witnesses, no alibis. Joseph had to
instantly see the hot water he was in. Although the passage
doesn't tell us if Potiphar's wife intentionally sent the others
away, I certainly wouldn't put it past her. To his credit,
Joseph made a practice of avoiding situations like the one

he was in. But when circumstances got out of control, he was left with only one solution....

5. Bolt like a bat.

Why did Joseph dash out of her inviting grasp? There's no such thing as playing "footsies" with a lit stick of dynamite. My rule of thumb: When communication and diplomacy fail, bail. That's the premise of 1 Corinthians 6:18, "Flee from sexual immorality." Don't think. Don't dawdle. Just do the holy hustle and get your butt out of there—pronto!

Tending the Goats on Mt. Gilead

In Song of Songs 4:1, the bridegroom describes his bride with colorful poetry: "How beautiful you are, my darling! Oh, how beautiful! Your eyes behind your veil are doves. Your hair is like a flock of goats descending from Mount Gilead." About those goats on Mount Gilead ... several years ago I was tending to a few of my own.

This was one of those informal evenings with a special female friend. Dinner and conversation, laughter, and a long walk. Truly an enjoyable night of innocent fun. Driving back to her apartment, Debbie told me she baked a pie for dessert. How thoughtful. We ate and talked in her living room.

> When communication and diplomacy fail, bail.

I come from a "touchy" family so back rubs are considered therapy—not a prelude to intimate acts. Those who know me know that I give anyone in need a relaxing neck massage. Evidently, I pushed a button with Debbie. Rather abruptly her conversation changed directions. "Stay with me tonight," she suggested.

Excuse me? Thinking quickly about everything that was said and done over the course of the evening, I couldn't understand where the sexual advance came from. Then it struck me. Debbie was a relatively new Christian who had engaged in premarital sex before coming to Christ. Maybe she was forgetting a few details about her new faith.

Frankly, she was a beautiful woman whom I thoroughly enjoyed being with. A debate in my brain kicked into high gear. On one hand I wanted to remind both of us that sex was not a biblical option. On the other hand, I heard, "What's wrong with you, Bob? You're crazy to deny yourself! At twenty-six isn't it about time to experience the pleasures of a woman? You're alone—nobody will know."

Thankfully, I listened to that still small voice whispering "Bob, remember where you draw the bottom line—don't cross it. Don't even get close. Flee." Respectfully, I communicated my position on the idea of premarital sex, then made plans to wind things down for the night. She persisted.

Walking to the door I thanked her for a wonderful evening. As I did, she leaned over and kissed me on the cheek. Think fast, Bob. "As much as I might like to reciprocate," I began, "if we start in that direction it will be difficult to stop."

Getting into my car, I heard Debbie try one last time. "It would be so nice to hear your voice in the morning next to me...."

As I learned years ago from Joseph, *now* was the time to bolt like a bat. No debate. No delay. Lingering was out— and so was I. Think back to my rule of thumb: "When communication and diplomacy fail, bail." This was the situation that gave birth to this profundity.

Several weeks later I had an opportunity to put into practice what I learned from my previous experience with Debbie. I should never have allowed myself to accept her late night invitation for dessert in the first place. I blew it and was determined not to make the same mistake again. Like Andrea, I was setting myself up for failure.

Her name was Kim. I met her at a local Christian radio

station where we worked together on a few special projects. Several weeks later I invited her to dinner. Approaching her driveway afterwards, Kim invited me to come inside for some "payback." As delightful as she was—and believe me she was attractive in the fullest sense of the word, I declined.

My close encounter with Deb was still fresh in my mind. It cautioned me not to take even one step in her direction. To go inside and have sex with someone who wasn't my wife simply would not be worth it. Sometimes it's best to allow the "goats on Mount Gilead" to graze peacefully alone.

Keep Your Eyes on Your Own Fries

Some people will do *anything* to keep their sexual drive from going into overdrive. Take, for instance, the chastity belt. Designed to be worn by a woman, this combination of metal plates and padlocks prevented access to the genitals. Too bad they didn't create one for the wayward-prone guy.

Besides the obvious problems with such an approach—not to mention the outright male hypocrisy—it was a short-sighted solution at best. How so? The belt concept views sexuality simply in terms of the plumbing. Guarding access to one's genitals offers no protection against affairs of the heart.

In reality, the act of sex is far more complicated than plumbing. It's entwined with the very core of our being. Dr. James Dobson describes the power of our sexual nature as "the energy that holds a people together."[2] God designed sex to blend our heart, soul, mind, *and* body in one special act reserved for marriage.

Sex is so intimate and so priceless we should guard it with more than a padlock. Furthermore, our commitment to enjoy sexual intimacy God's way versus man's way (chapter 3) is worth protecting with unswerving determination. But how? In addition to the five steps Joseph used to stay on track, let's look at several other valuable perspectives.

Remind yourself of the advantages of abstaining:

1. You sleep better with no regrets, fears, or guilt following you to bed.

2. Freedom from *all* sexually transmitted diseases. Wow! (That's an idea you and I can live with.)

3. Avoids unwanted memories in marriage, which better sets the stage for dynamic sex.

4. Retains higher level of confidence, self-worth, and self-esteem. Your value as a person is not tied to a passing sexual performance.

5. You walk through life knowing that your decision to abstain brings pleasure to your heavenly Father.

6. Disobedience of God's laws—including matters of sex—will hinder our prayer life. "God doesn't listen to the prayers of men who flout the law" (Prov. 28:9 LB).

7. Abstinence enables us to deepen the level of even casual conversations. No longer are we restricted to the shallowness of flirtatious sexual small talk—a mode of communication that frequently characterizes snakes on the make.

8. Abstaining enables you to nurture the other person. You can relax and approach all dates with the question "What can I *give*" rather than "What can I *get*" from this person.

9. Although I part company on a number of points with Dr. Gabrielle Brown, she does express my sentiments with this passage from her book, *The New Celibacy*:

> Just as silence is the basis for sound, for speech, for music, celibacy is the basis for sex. . . . If a person has been playing the stereo constantly for weeks and then turns it off one day, she immediately "hears" the silence, and that silence seems full. Listening more closely, she may even

hear in her own head some subtle music that is more charming than what she was listening to on the stereo all that time.

By being celibate, by turning off the "sexual stereo," one may discover a new dimension of response in love, in creation, in perception underneath the sexual program. People may then find that they are able to begin to experience a quality of attention that makes them more tuned in to feelings of intimacy, tenderness, and fullness of love in relationships, as well as in other parts of their lives.

Instead of being dominated by just one kind of human love—the sexual—they are free to experience other responses.[3]

Remember the realities of chastity:

1. Making a commitment to chastity will not cause you to lose your eyesight or your hair. Nor, contrary to the opinion of some, will you spontaneously explode. You've made a wise choice.

2. Remember: making a commitment to chastity is great, but your body doesn't know if you're married or single. It responds as it was designed to respond when faced with a stimulating situation. Do yourself a favor and avoid energizing your engines with music, magazines, films, or television shows that revel in racy raunch. Don't ignite fires you cannot put out.

3. Do you travel for a living? How will you handle hotel pornography? It's tough to do it alone—after all, what's a "harmless" five-minute free preview? Don't believe that lie for a second! Find an accountability partner and permit this confidant to quiz you upon your return about the viewing choices you made.

4. Protective eye-gear is highly recommended. Such was the practice of Job. He writes, "I made a covenant with

my eyes not to look lustfully at a girl" (Job 31:1). We live in a society of voyeurs who have lost the ability to avert the eye. Work at perfecting this lost art. Furthermore, in the eyes of this society, the only *abnormal* sex is engaging in *abstinence* until marriage—don't be blinded by that lie.

Remember the value of abstaining:

1. In 1994, *Redbook* magazine spearheaded a survey of 500 women on the question of premarital sex. It's hard to believe what they found. A whopping *64 percent* of those responding revealed the fact they "would want to be a *virgin* if they were getting married today."[4]

2. Nearly 1,000 subscribers to *Christianity Today* completed a survey on sexual satisfaction in marriage. The researchers found a clear link *between abstinence and sexual happiness in marriage.* Dr. David Larson reviewed the research and commented, "Couples not involved before marriage and faithful during marriage are more satisfied with their current sex life than those who were involved sexually before marriage."[5]

3. According to the 1994 Churched Youth Survey commissioned by Josh McDowell, three-quarters of churched teens claim that virginity would be their preferred sexual state at the time of marriage. And for good reason. The evidence demonstrates it's better when you wait. The deeper the commitment, the deeper the level of intimacy and arousal.[6]

No Guts, No Glory

Have you ever seen a palm tree? I mean actually viewed one in person? Living in Philadelphia most of my life, palm trees were what you might call a little scarce. I must have been in my mid-twenties before encountering one up close and personal. Whenever you finally catch up with this tropical wonder, inspect it closely. You'll discover a rather interesting feature.

Sitting proudly on top of a long pole-like trunk you'll notice the distinguishing brownish-green branches. Here's the fascinating part. The palm tree stands taller only when a part of it dies. Those crowning branches at the top must tumble to the ground, which is the only way to make room for new growth. Without the loss, there would be no gain.

The lesson?

When it comes to containing our volcanic sex drive, I'm not one to suggest it will be easy. Au contraire. It's tough work. Frankly, this notion that part of me must die in order for me to grow goes against my human nature. But as a single adult who longs for God's best, I daily choose to lay down my desires, my needs, my wants, and my drives.

> **In the eyes of this society, the only abnormal sex is engaging in abstinence until marriage.**

Doing so enables me—like the palm tree—to stand taller and reach new heights.

In like fashion, the world's finest wines require two things: crushed grapes and time. If the fruit of the vine refuses to be squeezed beyond recognition it will never join the ranks of a Dom Perignon classic. How are you responding to the wine press of restraint? Are you going with the flow or does your face portray "sour grapes"? Are you impatient with the bottling process?

Before popping your cork allowing everything to run loose, listen to the prayerful petition of Marjorie Holms:

To Live Without Sex

If I must live without sex, Lord, help me to do so gracefully. Don't let me become bitter and resentful, blaming you, the world, or anybody else. Instead of self-pity, give me the strength and the cheerful acceptance that comes from self-respect. Above all, give me understanding; the wisdom to sort out the complexities of this common human condition.

It's so easy to confuse what the body thinks it needs and wants with what the mind and the world dictate. Protect me from this confusion, Lord, don't let me be misled. Help me to remember, Lord, many people endure afflictions and deprivations far worse. And that a great many people live happy, purposeful, inspiring lives that are devoid of sex.

Give me their secrets of acceptance, give me their grace. If I am to live without sex, Lord, allow me to express and use this great force you have given me for some significant end.[7]

Speaking of intense sex drives, Marjorie desired to use "this great force" for "some significant end." After all, sexual dynamism *can* be properly channeled. How? I'm glad you asked. The next chapter provides fifty incredible nonsexual ways to divert this sexual energy. What's more, we'll practice becoming a godly lover and advance the kingdom in the process.

CHAPTER 7

Becoming a Great Lover

Genuine love is honor put into action, regardless of the cost. It comes from a heart overflowing with affection for God, freeing us to seek another person's best interest.

—*Gary Smalley and John Trent[1]*

My command is this: Love each other as I have loved you. Greater love has no one than this, that he lay down his life for his friends.

—*Jesus (John 15:12–13)*

*A*re you familiar with Calvin and Hobbes? Calvin is a young boy, probably six years of age. His active imagination finds him conversing with Hobbes—a stuffed tiger who comes to life in Calvin's head. Together, this dynamic duo explores life in the popular cartoon strip bearing their names.

In one charming episode, Calvin asks what's it like to fall in love. Thoughtfully, Hobbes responds, "Well . . . say the object of your affection walks by. First, your heart falls into your stomach and splashes your innards. All the moisture makes you sweat profusely." Calvin listens intently as the tiger continues.

"This condensation shorts the circuits to your brain and you get all woozy. When your brain burns out altogether, your mouth disengages, and you babble like a Cretin until she leaves," explains Hobbes. Calvin can't contain himself and shouts, "THAT'S LOVE?!?" "Medically speaking," Hobbes proudly proclaims. Calvin quietly considers his companion's conclusion. Calvin's response is classic: "Heck, that happened to ME once, but I figured it was cooties!"[2]

With a smile on my face I thought back to a similar question that super group Foreigner asked in the mid-eighties. The haunting chorus of this hit song repeatedly cried out, "I want to know what love is, I want you to show me." As Foreigner sang, millions of fans identified with their longing. Why? Demonstrations of genuine love are few and far between.

Just look at the stuff that comes out of Hollywood. Film and television producers have conveniently narrowed the definition of love, viewing it principally in terms of Eros— the erotic: love = sex; sex = love. They've elected to see it as a one-dimensional act. After all, it's an easy sell—and we're tempted to buy the line.

Actually the word *eros* doesn't appear anywhere in the New Testament. When Jesus said that the most important commandment is to love the Lord your God with all of your heart, soul, strength, and mind, and to love your neighbor as yourself (Mark 12:29–31), the word he used for love was *agape*. Whether describing God's great love for us—or commanding us to love one another—*agape* is the only form of love used in the New Testament.

At the outset of this book I stated that marriage and sex should not be our objective—rather, becoming a godly lover is the goal. Such was the case in the life of Christ. If we're to become more Christlike, we'll need to learn that generosity and serving others is at the heart of the matter. In so doing, we'll best prepare ourselves for life whether we remain single or married.

50 Ways to Be a Lover

As the old story goes, there once was a man who shouted in the bar, "When I drink, everybody drinks!" Throughout the tavern a spontaneous cheer broke out. Wow, what a kind man! After emptying his glass, the boisterous benefactor hopped onto a bar stool and proclaimed, "When I have another drink, everybody has another drink!" A rousing cheer accompanied the second round of drinks.

After finishing this second beer, the man leaped onto the bar. "And when I pay," the man stated slapping $5 into the bartender's cup, "everybody pays!"

Generosity.

How few of us know how to exemplify it! I'm not speaking of benevolence strictly in the sense of our finances, although that's a part of it. Generosity as a godly lover means actually giving of our*selves*. It means backing up our words with real-life service. Godly lovers recognize the giant chasm between showing love and showing concern and work to bridge the gap with their actions.

The primary difference between love and concern is in the depth of giving of yourself. It's got substance, and it's more than a symbolic gesture. Watch how these two words stack up against each other, and ask yourself which quality you tend to gravitate towards:

CONCERN	LOVE
Superficial	Sacrificial
Verbalizes	Acts
Lip service	Life service
Minimal effort	Goes the extra mile
From your head	From your heart
Evaluates, sometime acts	Acts, sometime evaluates

"Hope your finances work out."	"Here's $50, hope it helps."
"How's your sick child doing?"	"Try this medicine, it works."
"Hope you fix that tire."	"Here, let me assist you."
"Car won't start? Call AAA."	"Why don't you borrow mine?"

The apostle John gets almost aggressive on this matter of demonstrating Christlike love, a love that moves well beyond a mere show of concern. Listen to the passion in his words:

> We know what real love is from Christ's example in dying for us. And so we also ought to lay down our lives for our Christian brothers. Little children, let us stop just *saying* we love people; let us *really* love them, and *show it* by our *actions*. (1 John 3:16, 18 LB, emphasis added)

It's better to do something for someone rather than just to offer. Because when you offer, it allows the person an opportunity to decline. Many decline out of embarrassment, not because their need isn't genuine. Others are not used to being considered worthy of another's generosity. Don't allow these apprehensions to stop you from exercising your love.

Do you desire to become a godly lover? Are you willing to put your talents, your resources, and your heart into action? Great. But where to begin? You might not see yourself as the imaginative type and perhaps you feel strapped for good ideas. No problem.

I've assembled fifty fun, rewarding, and practical ways to practice loving others as God would have us love them. You'll find a wide range of ideas to implement throughout the year. Some are simple, others are more involved. Several suggestions will cost you nothing more than your creative brain space and postage. Others span the range from inexpensive to hundreds of dollars.

You'll notice most can be managed by yourself, while a small group lending a hand will work best in a few instances. The key is to learn how to give—and how to enjoy doing it without drawing attention to yourself in the process. As you get going, you'll soon see how enriched your life becomes. Isn't it about time we stop talkin' and start walkin'?

1. Don't Whine, Shine!

Approaching the kitchen, your mind flashes back to biology class. The dishes stacked to the ceiling contain enough bacteria to give a scientist indigestion. The next time you attack the stack, wash your roommates' dishes after you finished with your own. Put a little shine on those pots, too. Then leave a note: "Compliments of the U.S. Health Department."

2. Wake Up and Smell the Coffee

A personal favorite is to make my parents breakfast on Saturday morning—and serve it to them in bed! Homemade sweet rolls or fresh baked muffins, O. J., and coffee or tea served on a tray would even put a grin on the Mona Lisa. Placing a daisy or carnation alongside the plates is the perfect touch. Wanna freak out your roommate—this is the perfect dish.

3. Coffee to Go

Feeling adventuresome? Try the same treat on an unsuspecting buddy. My friend Phil was getting married. On the morning of his wedding, I brought the spread to his bed. Although I forgot about it, he reminded me ten years later!

4. Going the Extra Yard

You notice your neighbors' grass is starting to get taller

than their shrubs. How about a quick trim when you see they're out?

5. Giving Notice

Everyone can use a word of encouragement from time to time. Consider stashing little notes of appreciation in a friend's car, pantry, desk drawer—even his or her coat pocket. Signed or unsigned, the thought will count!

6. Dare to Baby Care

Some married couples—especially those with infants and small children—find it difficult to afford a sitter. Why not provide them with a night off and give them a break from the action. In turn, you'll get a head start polishing your parenting skills. I know a guy who sits for a couple in his church once a week ... he's prepared to have ten of his own!

7. Santa in September

Unemployed. What a distressing word—especially for the family whose breadwinner feels like burnt toast. Do you know someone who is without work? Don't wait for the holidays to lend a hand. Go "power shopping" for their basics (pasta, soup, cereal, fruit, yes—even the toilet paper). In fact, you may want to concentrate your shopping spree on nonfood items—paper products, laundry detergent, shampoo, and soap. Why? If the family has access to food stamps they won't be permitted to spend them on these types of nonfood essentials. Drop by with your little delivery and watch their spirits soar! I've enjoyed doing this for families when I was able to slip in and out of their house unannounced.

8. Flowers to Go

Back in college, someone gently tucked a tiny yellow

buttercup flower under my car's windshield wiper. At the end of a tough day, I hopped into the car and drove off. Only then did I notice this well-placed gift. To this day I still don't know who the angel was that demonstrated this act of thoughtfulness. My editor told me she once had someone tuck a dollar bill under her windshield wiper—a most memorable surprise.

9. The Perfect Word

We're quick to give hurting friends our opinion or advice. If only we were as speedy to share an insight from the Scriptures. I'm not talking about a sermon—just a verse or two that speaks to their situation. It's amazing to see how powerful the Word of God is in every imaginable circumstance.

10. Music to the Ears

Maybe I'm just a frustrated disc jockey, but I've always enjoyed assembling a cassette tape of favorite Christian love songs for a special friend. Weaving a few "warm fuzzy" comments in between the tunes is a nice touch. (Just go easy on the heavy breathing.)

11. Whispered Thoughts

Speaking of tapes, I remember receiving a cassette that contained quiet biblical reflections. A girlfriend softly read the writings of one of my favorite authors—Chuck Swindoll. Throughout the reading, she'd pause to add a few "insights for living" of her own. What a precious treasure!

12. Power of the Press

With the advent of desktop publishing, here's an idea that's relatively easy to produce. Using a page layout program, design the front page of a homespun newspaper. Best of all, the editorial slant lies in your hands. Of course, you could use your publication to playfully ask someone for a date! I can see the headlines: "Most Eligible Bachelor Requests Presence of _____ Tonight."

13. Pretzels: A New Twist to Encouragement

Being raised in Philadelphia accounts for my addiction to jumbo soft pretzels. Having located a local source for premium twists here in Colorado Springs, I arranged to purchase one hundred of these heavenly delights at wholesale. For fun I walked around the office where I worked, passing them out to my coworkers. As I delivered each I added a simple word of appreciation for their efforts. Guys, it's also a great way to meet new women!

14. Sign of the Times

My family has always been big on homemade banners. Mother's Day. Anniversaries. Accomplishments. Encouragements. Birthdays. Homecomings. We'd make these bold placards for each other and hang them throughout the house. The tradition continued for me even with my roommates at college. They, of course, thought it was a requirement for Advertising 101. To this day we "wallpaper" our home with custom posters.

15. Wheels of Fortune

His name was Saul. While he was out of town a thief stole all four of his car tires. Having limited resources and no insurance to replace them, Saul was going nowhere fast. Thankfully, the story has a happy spin. An observant coworker collected money from everyone at the office to contribute for new wheels. Also, if you see a friend riding on threadbare tires, see if you can "spare" some change.

16. Shovel It

As kids living in Philadelphia we were always looking

for ways to make some extra cash. In the winter we'd go door-to-door and offer to shovel driveways and sidewalks for the exorbitant sum of a whole dollar. Why not blaze the trails today—and skip the dollar! Note to my readers in Hawaii: don't hold your breath for this opportunity.

17. A Constructive Idea

How handy are you with a hammer and wrench? Next time you're visiting a single parent, look around. See that leaky faucet in the kitchen? How about the loose floorboards on the back porch or the toilet seat that's seen a better life? Mentally make a list of what needs to be done and what you can responsibly handle. Don't ask—just fix it when you come back. Even replacing burned-out lightbulbs is a bright option.

18. Just the Fax, Ma'am

Hey, it's the nineties. What's life like without a fax machine? Several members of my family have home faxes, which we use to zip notes of encouragement back and forth. And when I travel, a fax is usually waiting for me at the hotel—talk about a nice touch from home. Don't happen to have a fax machine handy? Try a convenience or packaging store. There you can send a fax to a friend at work or who's traveling. Incidentally, my mom applies her lipstick and actually kisses her faxes before sending them!

19. Run for the Border

Surely you've noticed a friend working all day without having time for lunch. Bag a burrito from Taco Bell and drop it off at his desk when he's stepped away. Don't forget the hot sauce!

20. Rake and Run

Here's an easy fall workout for you and a couple of

friends. Grab your rakes and trash bags. Target several homes that you know could use the help with the fallen leaves in their yard—perhaps where the occupant is elderly, bedridden, or just plain old exhausted. Without asking, rake the leaves then run to the next home.

21. Drive-by Witness

Are you aware of a woman who is subjected to spousal abuse? Place a Bible with a kind note on her doorstep. Consider gathering addresses and phone numbers of nearby shelters and tuck them into the card. If appropriate, reach out to her with a pastoral visit.

22. Color Her World

Guys, if I've learned anything about women, I've come to understand how much they appreciate great-looking nails. Why not spring for a manicure or a heavenly pedicure? Find out if and where your special lady gets her nails done, then purchase a certificate for the full treatment. Of course, both men and women can enjoy doing this for a single mom.

23. Hey, Mr. Postman

Are you aware of someone who is experiencing an especially difficult time? Maybe they're sick, separated, on the verge of a divorce, or there's been a death in the family. Whatever the reason, mail them a different card every day for one week expressing your love and support. This is also a great idea even when troubling times are not in sight.

24. Bag It

Most supermarkets and party goods stores sell little paper bags with colorful prints on the sides and two handles on top. Fill the bag with candy and gum. Toss in a small packet of bubble bath and a note. Then hang the bag on someone's apartment or dorm room door. The whole thing might cost five dollars, but it will make a priceless impression.

25. "Operation E"

When was the last time you did something to encourage your pastor? Offer to watch his kids to give him an evening out. Maybe slip an anonymous dinner-for-two gift certificate into the offering plate with his name on it. Tickets so he can take the family to a ballgame are also a welcome treat. (I'd probably stay away from sending him lottery tickets!)

26. Tooling Around

Tire pressure. Anti-freeze, oil, and transmission fluid levels. Headlights, taillights, interior lights. We're talking auto mechanics for beginners. With our busy lifestyles, few take the time to cover the basics. Give a friend's car the royal treatment . . . throwing in a wash, vacuum, and thirty-nine-cent air freshener will make their ride feel like it's brand new.

27. Baby Talk

So you'd like to have a baby. Only one obstacle: you're still single. No problem. Find someone who just gave birth and spoil their little angel as if it were your own. They'll probably need baby bottles, blankets, toys, food, wipes, powder, and a small truckload of diapers. I did this the other day—talk about a reality check on the cost of kid supplies!

28. Mother's Morning Out

Most of us view baby-sitting only in terms of an evening necessity. Of equal, if not greater, importance is child care during the morning. College students might consider adopting a mom for a month. Bring your books over once or twice a week to study while she takes the morning to do her errands or her aerobics.

29. Hotel California

I knew a couple that was working virtually seven days a week. Their long grueling hours had them pushed to the limit. When their anniversary rolled around, I provided a complimentary overnight stay at a local hotel. Utilizing several of the above ideas, I decorated their room with posters, a treat bag, and bubble bath tray.

30. Certify Your Love

It can be as simple as a five dollar book of McDonald gift coupons or as wonderful as a ski-lift certificate. There is virtually an endless number of ways to declare your love and care with gift certificates. Sometimes the small "free" ones are best: "This certificate entitles the bearer to a complimentary foot massage."

31. Food for Thought

I imagine somebody somewhere once said, "Poetry is the food of love." Expressing yourself in a handwritten poem makes a big impression. Attaching a miniature dried flower to it by your signature speaks volumes.

32. Card Games

Have you discovered the self-design card machines at places like Wal-Mart, K-Mart, or the mall? Thanks to computer technology you can custom make a card featuring a wide variety of lovable cartoon characters (Daffy Duck, Tweety Bird, Charlie Brown, and the like) expressing *your* script. Sure beats the "I miss you," "Get well soon," or "Be my Valentine" boring, generic, and unimaginative drivel contained in most store-bought cards.

33. Loafing Around

I don't know what it's like to spend my final days on earth in a retirement center for the elderly—especially when it comes to the food service. Even in the best extended care facilities the institutional food must get a tad boring. Why not use some Sunday afternoons to bake and deliver fresh bread to those who haven't seen the real thing in ages.

34. Thirst Quenchers

Next time you head to the cafeteria for something to drink, think of one other person you could treat.

35. Adventures in Odyssey

Focus on the Family has created a fantastic radio drama series for children called "Adventures in Odyssey." This wildly popular program has been captured on cassette tape. Over the years I've supplied the children of several families with the latest from the land of Odyssey. It sure makes baby-sitting smoother and helps us single adults better relate to the little ones.

36. A Date with Mr. Clean

I have calculated that Mom and Dad served me 10,953 meals between the ages of seven and seventeen! Preferring home cooking, we were not a clan that ate meals out very often. No wonder my parents got gray hair. I figure the least I could do is to play the part of Mr. Clean's White Tornado when I visit home. Bathrooms. Closets. Bedrooms. Counter tops. Dusting. Vacuuming under *everything*. The housework is endless. Oh, Mom keeps a wonderful house. But everyone can use a break from the daily struggle fighting dust. Besides, it's good practice for marriage.

37. Iron Will

When it comes to hygiene and personal wardrobe, we guys can be a sorry bunch. Interestingly, I don't recall meeting a guy in college who owned an iron. But I do remember a precious coed once took it upon herself to iron my shirts and hang them by my laundry basket . . . that was either an act of kindness or a serious hint!

38. Great Clips

Articles. Photos. Reports. Recipes. I've always appreciated it when a friend learns of my interest in a particular topic and proceeds to collect these items on my behalf. I now find myself doing the same thing for others. When I come across something of value, I'll attach a simple yellow post-it note to the surface and forward it (or fax it) to the friend who can put it to good use.

39. Now Read This!

From time to time I'm able to do more than an occasional clipping. Michelle mentioned her interest in decorating her home Victorian style. The following week at the bookstore I noticed a Victorian magazine containing numerous inexpensive Victorian decor tips. I mailed it to her.

40. More Than Hot Air

Notice a coworker having a tough day? During lunch swing by a florist. Instead of springing for flowers, try floating a colorful bunch of giant balloons over his desk. Keep in mind a growing number of party supply stores have the ability to custom inscribe a name on these inflatables.

41. Get a Mug Mug

Here's a hot idea. Warm the heart of a friend with a coffee cup that has a mug shot of you both on it. Specialty shops now offer this photographic novelty.

42. Advertise Your Love

Have a friend who's down in the dumps? How about a cherished confidante that you'd like to do something crazy for? Why not buy one thirty second commercial on a local Christian radio station and deliver a special message to her? Ask the station to run it during the morning drive. Then tell your friend to tune in on the day it's scheduled to air. In the majority of cities around the country, you'd only have to pay about twenty-five to thirty-five dollars and can record the commercial with your voice in their studios!

43. Unleash the Cookie Monster

Make a giant cookie with a sweet message on it for your friend. This will kill all attempts at losing weight, but will surely bring a smile. (When I say "giant" I'm talking at least a foot in diameter.) Hate to bake? Local bake shops do this for a living. Leave the cookie on her desk or the front seat of his car. You could always place it wrapped decoratively on the doorstep, ring the bell, and disappear.

44. Love Notes

Most of these ideas are not designed solely for use within a dating relationship, although they certainly serve that purpose. This, however, is one that's best used between those in a committed relationship. Purchase a fine grade of stationary and hand write a letter expressing the depth of your love. Don't rush it, and skip the corny mush. It may be something your grandchildren read one day!

45. Soul Food

Recently, a friend was struggling with low self-esteem. In the past, I've dashed out to the store and purchased a book to help with the problem—be it fear, anxiety, sex, or past memories. This time I took an afternoon to write a simple Bible study that we could work on together. By creating my own guide, I was able to personalize it.

46. Flower Power

Buy a dozen flowers—roses, daisies—it doesn't matter the variety. Over dinner, present the flowers one at a time. With each describe an attribute or quality that you appreciate about your guest.

47. Postcards from the Edge

Write a letter that concludes with a fun bottom line: Meet me at the mall. Be there the last Tuesday of this month at noon for lunch—my treat. Then, divide the letter into twelve short segments that you transfer onto twelve postcards. Mail the cards one a day leading up to the creative date.

48. Party Hardy

Everybody celebrates their birthday on the date of their birth. Why not dedicate one *entire week* either before or after the actual date and do something special each day. A cake, flowers, a huge card—allow your creative juices to fill their seven-day celebration.

49. Foot Magic

For that special person in your life, pull out a foot massage machine and fill it with hot water. Pour in a package of Johnson's Foot Powder and let the magic begin! You can walk the extra mile if you know how to give a pedicure.

50. Strawberry Surprise

I must admit that I met my creative match the other day in California. After speaking to a large crowd for several hours, I retired to my hotel. Upon entering my room, I saw a tray of fresh strawberries and whipped cream! Apparently, someone from the seminar ordered and paid for this room service treat ... a kind gesture I'll never forget.

~ ❦ ~

Don't Forget About Treating Yourself!

As I reviewed this wide array of options, an important thought came to mind. I'm not suggesting you and I focus on other people while routinely ignoring our personal and emotional needs for a loving touch. There are definitely times when we need to bask in a special treat for ourselves. A leisurely bath. Getting lost in a long novel. Wading through a stack of classic movie videos. Buying that new outfit. Lingering over a secluded dinner at a fine restaurant. Or "splurging" on a private blend of tea while munching on a favorite snack.

As I've mentioned previously, learning to be our own best friend—to enjoy our own company—is important now and will serve us well in marriage. These ideas represent practical measures we can embrace to celebrate our own company. I've also found that taking time for myself helps to prevent my slipping into the quagmire of self-pity and the poor choices we discussed in chapter 5. What's more, taking a mini-sabbatical from time to time enables us to be refreshed when we reach out to touch the lives of others.

Valentine's Day ... Have a Heart

February 14.

Unlike real holidays, Valentine's Day must have been concocted by the card and chocolate companies to bolster their sagging spring sales. Gregory Godek, author of *1001 Ways to be Romantic*, describes this holiday as "one of those *Obligatory Romance* days." Even so he advises, "you still have to recognize it and act on it—but you don't get any extra credit for it, guys."[3]

It's one of the busiest days of the year for florists. At the same time, for many singles it's a quiet day of bitter reflection. I asked the singles in my survey to describe what is typically their emotional state on February 14. As you'll see from this representative sample, it's a story of extremes. Either happiness abounds and life is worth living, or they're mostly dead.

How about you? Is Cupid a pain in the butt or an angel of the highest order?

Kim: I *hate* Valentine's Day! I generally spend the entire day (and several surrounding days) in a state of aggravated, artificial PMS!

Steve: I want to bury my head for a day. It just compounds the hurt. I would love to have someone to send flowers to and treat to a romantic dinner. As I watch each flower delivery, my heart gets more and more bitter.

Mary: I reflect on happy memories, recalling the flowers, cards and chocolate I've received, the fun dinners that were shared. Even though I don't always get the treatment, life's too short to mope around.

Mack: I get pretty down. It's an intense day for me with few memories. I wonder why not me? It's the Lord's love that keeps me steady.

Jane: Usually blissful because I've always had someone up until now. This year looks like the pits and I'll probably end up in tears.

Greg: I tune in to the soft hits station and listen to them play love songs and dream about how nice it would be to have someone. Then I stick my head out the window and bark at the moon!

Rhoda: Wonderful! My boyfriend is so thoughtful. He never fails to surprise me with special treats on Valentine's Day.

Betty: Lonely, depressed, and a bit envious of friends who receive gifts from their significant other.

Robert: Lousy. You might say it sucks canal water. I'd like
    to stay in bed all day and call radio stations to dedicate
    J. Geils' "Love Stinks" and Phil Collins' "I Don't Care
    Anymore" to my old girlfriends.

Personally speaking, I've always tried to make the most
of the day. Yes, it hasn't always been a box of chocolate.
Take, for instance, the first time I discussed the topic of this
book with several staff members from my publishing company. We were having dinner together in a cozy restaurant
in Los Angeles—on Valentine's Day! How ironic. A book
on sex and the single person conceived on February 14. God
certainly has an interesting sense of humor!

Just as we've been looking at ways to act as a godly lover
throughout the year, there are several options to make this
a happier "holiday" for all concerned. For instance, I once
purchased two dozen roses on Valentine's Day and walked
around the office leaving one on the work station of my single coworkers. You should have seen the smiles!

I've heard reports of singles who have hosted a party in
their home for their single friends. Or you could play the
"secret admirer" and mail an anonymous valentine to several
that could use one. And rather than sit at home calling radio
stations with sour dedications, why not invite your brother
or sister out for a fun, informal evening.

The bottom line: giving ought to be a way of life for the
godly lover. He or she will work overtime to enrich the lives
of those around them. With practice this art of giving
becomes second nature.

Finally, don't be turned off when you don't get the
thanks you think you deserve. For a godly lover, it's the giving that counts, not the thanks you get for it. After all,
you're really supposed to be doing these acts of kindness as
unto the Lord. (See parable in Matthew 25:34–46.)

I've discovered that over time you will actually begin to

look at people and their needs as an opportunity to extend Christ's love. Best of all, you enter into the fullness of the meaning of his promise, "It is more blessed to give than to receive" (Acts 20:35). So why not take a run at a few of these ideas and watch what a difference it makes in *you*!

I Wanna Hold Your Hand

We've been discussing nonsexual ways to demonstrate and experience love, care, and affection. Next, we turn our attention to a fascinating examination of dating and mating in the shadow of the AIDS crisis. It's a real eye-opener that is sure to radically change the way you approach the selection of a potential mate.

To set the stage, let's test your knowledge of sexually transmitted diseases with four questions:

1. Assuming proper application, how often do condoms fail when blocking the HIV virus?
   a. 2 percent of the time.
   b. 10 percent of the time.
   c. 15 percent of the time.
   d. 31 percent of the time.
2. How many diseases that can be sexually transmitted have been identified today?
   a. About five.
   b. Less than fifteen.
   c. About twenty-five.
   d. More than fifty.
3. What ratio accurately represents the number of adult Americans who now are infected with a permanent STD?
   a. 1 in 10,000.
   b. 1 in 1,000.

    c. 1 in 100.

    d. 1 in 4.

4. True or false: Sexually transmitted diseases can be passed through French kissing.

For the correct answers, join me in the next chapter. Oh, you better be sitting down! What you'll learn may surprise you.

PART THREE

Dating in the Nineties: Applying Intimacy, Avoiding Disease

CHAPTER 8

Before You Kiss, Read This

There's nothing wrong with going to bed with somebody of your own sex. People should be free with sex—they should draw the line at goats.

—*Elton John, British singer[1]*

Those who suggest such "radical notions" as chastity before marriage and faithfulness in marriage are told that these approaches are too puritanical. The Puritans may have had some problems, but AIDS wasn't one of them.

—*Cal Thomas[2]*

It was a rainy Saturday night and I was in the mood to watch a classic love story. Scanning the video titles, I selected *It's A Wonderful Life*. Popcorn in hand, fire crackling nicely in its place, I was set. As the story unfolded, there was a timeless moment when Jimmy Stewart gazed into the sparkling eyes of Donna Reed.

The evening sky behind these lovebirds was softly accented by the glistening moonlight. In a moment of tenderness, Stewart proclaimed his budding love with an offer to lasso the moon and serve it to her on a silver platter. So uncomplicated. So innocent. So unlike the nineties!

Admit it, love and romance was a simpler matter in days

gone by. Today, if Jimmy and Donna wanted to get serious, I imagine the scene would have to be rewritten:

Jimmy: Oh Donna, I'd love to lasso the moon and serve it to you on a silver platter.

Donna: Yes, my love. But first, have you ever taken an AIDS test? How about your sexual history?

Jimmy: Huh?

Donna: Yeah, you know. What can you tell me about each of your previous lovers—and their lovers?

A far-fetched scenario? Hardly.

Welcome to the nineties where mate selection is a very different proposition. The days of innocence in the dating game are long gone. Why? AIDS and the rampant spread of numerous sexually transmitted diseases (STDs) demand that we change the way we select and relate to a date. Nowadays it's downright stupid to race into relationships with the speed of Mario Andretti at the Indianapolis 500.

Innocence of the facts is no longer bliss.

I must confess I've been driven into relationships when Cupid's arrow shot me in the heart. Instead of using my mind, I allowed the electric feelings inside of me to lead the way. Granted, part of the nature of love includes a certain degree of magnetism that defies logic. In the nineties, however, I've learned that when Cupid takes aim I *must* use my head in matters of the heart.

Here's an example of what I mean.

I've asked hundreds of singles, "Would you marry someone who tested HIV positive?" Almost without exception, the answer was a resounding "No way!" Frankly, after giving it much thought I don't believe I could either. I'm all for "'til death do us part." However, going into marriage with a mate who has a head start on the "death" part sounds a lot like suicide—not to mention an infected spouse would put a serious damper on your sexual intimacy as a couple.

How about you? Would you *marry* someone with AIDS—a fatal and contagious disease?

If not, there's a related question you ought to consider: Would you seriously *date* someone who was a carrier for the AIDS virus? After all, what

> Nowadays, it's downright stupid to race into relationships with the speed of Mario Andretti.

would be the point? If you've determined that you could not marry one who was HIV positive, does it make sense to spend the time, money, and emotional energy developing a relationship that has no real future?

Regardless of how you answered these questions, you can begin to see the quandary we singles are in. At no other point in the history of humankind has finding a mate taken on potentially deadly proportions. Catch AIDS and you will die sooner than later. No exceptions.

But the problem with STDs doesn't stop at this killer virus. Two out of three newborns who pick up a herpes infection from their mothers at birth will die, and most of the rest will be seriously handicapped.[3] In other words, STDs carry with them implications for the children you may one day desire to have.

I don't mean to sound like an alarmist, and there's certainly no reason to withdraw from the human race. But the wise single won't be afraid to ask tough questions of all serious marital candidates.

In this chapter we'll consider the crucial questions that *need* to be asked of any serious dating partners pertaining to their sexual history. We'll also consider how, and at what point, we should inquire about a sweetheart's previous sexual experiences. Then there's the tricky one: How would you ask a date to go get an AIDS test if he or she is not a virgin? We'll see what other singles have to say.

At no other point in the history of mankind has finding a mate taken on potentially deadly proportions.

I imagine there will be a number of readers who think this study is a bit of an overreaction. After all, haven't sexually transmitted diseases been around for centuries? Besides, many in the medical community have assured us that a properly applied condom is the Great Plastic Savior—one that covers a multitude of past sexual sins.

Is that so? Are condoms a one

CALVIN AND HOBBES ©1986 Watterson. Dist. by Universal Press Syndicate.
Reprinted by permission. All rights reserved.

hundred percent dependable solution? If they are, it hardly matters what wild diseases are running in the veins of our date. When we get married, we'd just have to always use one. On the other hand, if condoms aren't fully trustworthy, then sexual history as it applies to our mate selection cannot be overlooked.

We'll get the straight scoop from two highly respected doctors. In fact, that's an excellent place to start.

Postcards from the Past

Walking into the doctor's office, Sue thought her visit would be a routine checkup. Little did she know she was about to learn that the herpes virus was now a permanent member of her bloodstream. Upon receiving the news, all she could think was that her last sexual intercourse was several years ago. Like a postcard from the past, Sue was given a painful reminder of one short-lived fling.

It's worth pointing out that for two entire years she had no idea that she was a carrier of herpes. She experienced no external signs. As far as she was concerned, that particular expression of passion was old news. To look at her, you'd be tempted to agree. On the surface Sue appeared to be unblemished, but in reality her appeal was skin deep.

I relay that true story for a reason. When it comes to STDs, things are not always as they may appear. The people you and I select to date may have no outwardly visible signs of disease. In fact women, the guys you date may have Schwarzenegger-sized muscles. Or guys, you may go on a date with a lady who is as picture perfect as Cindy Crawford.

But in both cases it would be naive to assume all is well. Nor would it be prudent to assume a discussion about past sexual choices would be unnecessary.

Where, then, do we turn for sound advice?

I respect the medical insight of Dr. Joe McIlhaney. Based in Austin, Texas, this world-renowned specialist

The wise single won't be afraid to ask tough questions of all serious marital candidates.

began his obstetrical/gynecological practice almost three decades ago. I've had the privilege of getting to know Joe over the years and as an OB/GYN, you might say he understands STDs from the inside out. Let's start with a few basics.

In his book, *Sexuality and Sexually Transmitted Diseases* (Baker Books) the doctor defines a sexually transmitted disease as: "An infectious condition that is passed from one person to another during sexual activity."[4] He explains that the "principal transmission is through intimate sexual contact (including oral/genital contact, anal intercourse, and even 'French kissing') or through the use of contaminated I.V. needles."[5]

Not so fast . . . did our physician friend identify "French kissing" as a conduit for sexually transmitted disease? Yikes! I guess the next time my hot date says, "Kiss me," I may have to clarify what kind of kissing she has in mind!

The first time I read that statement an interesting thought struck me. The sexual playground of the sixties, which you and I have inherited, is now an explosive minefield. So much for the "Make Love, Not War" anthem of my bell bottom-clad hippie ancestors. To borrow a biblical expression, the sins of the fathers have been passed on to the third and fourth generations.

Today, when it comes to love in America, we're very much at war. Personally, as a single male seeking a mate in the nineties I'd like to know what I'm up against. I'm sure you do, too. Let's review the medical facts. See if these realities don't just slap you across the face:

- A short thirty years ago, the average health education course in high school discussed only *two* STDs: gonorrhea and syphilis.[6]

- By contrast, today there are more than *fifty* different organisms and syndromes which are passed sexually.[7]
- A lethal disease can be transmitted by a *single* sexual contact with *one* infected partner.[8] (Remember, that would include French kissing.)
- At least thirty percent of single, sexually active Americans have herpes.[9] This amounts to more than twenty million infected Americans as of 1993.[10]
- The herpes virus is spreading at the alarming rate of 500,000 new cases per year.[11]
- The venereal wart virus is carried by approximately thirty percent of single, sexually active adults.[12]
- Chlamydia has infected thirty to forty percent of sexually active young adults.[13]
- More than 33,000 new cases of a sexually transmitted disease are reported every day in America, according to statistics released by the Centers for Disease Control and Prevention in Atlanta.
- *56 million Americans* are infected with a permanent sexually transmitted disease.[14] Translation: approximately *one in four* of the adult population in our country now has a permanent STD.

> The sexual playground of the sixties which you and I have inherited is now an explosive minefield.

Those, dear reader, are the cold hard facts.

Unfortunately, facts frequently fail to prevail when the urge to merge surges. If possessing a knowledge of the facts worked, far more Americans would have been embracing the tightly zippered life over the years. And, I might add, this entire discussion wouldn't be necessary today.

Allow me to digress for a moment.

I'm making an assumption. You've heard me say sex and

marriage is not the goal—becoming a godly lover is. Further, I've made it clear we can approach intimacy man's way or God's way. And I've explained what's involved in becoming a great lover, as well as how to affirm others in nonsexual ways. My assumption is that you agree and long to find a mate who shares in your commitment to be a Christlike helpmate.

But such a sweeping presupposition is sure to be presumptuous on my part. Why? I fully realize that you may look at the facts and decide sex for you is just too darn important. You see the use of condoms as an acceptable risk. That's the way all of your friends operate, so you disagree that casual sex with condoms is gambling with your life.

If that's the case, this next section is as much for you as it is for the chaste reader.

Condom Mania

During the week of December 5, 1994, I was flipping the dial and landed on MTV during a commercial break. The Sheik prophylactic company was peddling their plastic wares to the young MTV audience. In this spot, a shaggy-haired teen sporting the "grunge" look went on a verbal rampage about why he would never wear a condom. His girlfriend, interrupting this diatribe, hands him a Sheik condom and informs him that he either wears one or he can forget about having sex with her.

Fifty-six million Americans are infected with a permanent sexually transmitted disease.

Instantly, the juvenile changes his tune and begins to say condoms are a wonderful thing. At the time this commercial aired, the reigning Condom Queen was ex-Surgeon General Joycelyn Elders. She must have been proud.

Speaking of Elders, what do this disastrous former Surgeon General, Madonna (another public embarrassment), and Ann Landers have in common? They advocate the use of condoms. Say what? Elders and Madonna I can understand. But the semi-saintly Ann Landers? Talk about odd bedfellows. Read what Landers stated in her highly acclaimed, syndicated newspaper column:

> I stand by my statement that "for some, abstinence is not a realistic alternative." . . . Self-control is certainly a virtue, but unfortunately, it often fails when confronted with the urge to merge. While condoms are certainly not fail-safe, they are a lot better than nothing (September 26, 1994).

Permit me a healthy gag, Ann.

Sounds like Landers has been studying the writings of Graham Masterton in her free moments. This former editor of *Penthouse* purports to have written some of the most popular sex manuals of all time. He's authored five books. His most recent effort, *Single, Wild, Sexy . . . and Safe*, delivers 248 pages of titillating sex stories that appeal to the prurient interest of peeping toms.

Regarding safe sex, Masterton dedicates a scant two and a half pages to the topic. He, like Landers, recommends the use of condoms. Listen to his ludicrous perspective: "There are plenty of single women who have overcome their social isolation . . . They have found lasting [!] sexual happiness [!!] . . . they have learned to live contentedly by themselves, taking lovers as and when they want them. It can be done, and you can do it"[15] (exclamations added).

You see, it's a short step between Landers' perspective—that self-control is difficult to sustain—and Masterton's "taking lovers" whenever you want philosophy. These two beliefs are actually kissing

Approximately one in four of the adult population in our country now has a permanent STD.

cousins. Both dismiss the role of morality and dismiss the virtue of chastity when questions of sex arise.

Masterton continues to define his position on sex. He writes, "Let me put my own sexual philosophy into one sentence: If it excites you, if it brings you happiness and satisfaction, and if nobody is hurt or put at risk, either physically or emotionally—then do it."[16]

But what about those nasty little letters H, I, and V?

On that issue, Masterton feels your pain: "One of the most inhibiting factors when you're looking for a new lover is the fear that he may be HIV-positive."[17] Amazing. Such insight. But what's a poor promiscuous person supposed to do?

"The single most effective protection against the transmission of AIDS is the condom … these days, you should never feel embarrassed about insisting that your lover wear a condom."[18] He recommends placing a large dish filled with an assortment of colorful condoms on your bed stand, "rather like a dish of jellybeans."

Yeah, you just never know who might swing by.

With a gospel-like flare, Masterton preaches the good news to the faithless: "You can protect yourself and prevent the spread of AIDS if you *always* use a condom when you have sex with somebody whose sexual history is questionable."[19]

Wrong-o, pal.

Has this guy taken a vacation from reality or what? And how about our dear Ann Landers. Sounds like she's taken a permanent cruise on the same Love Boat with Mr. sex-on-the-brain Masterton. Simply put, following their advice will get you an ugly STD souvenir at best—or, worse, killed.

Start with Landers' assertion that self-control is difficult to sustain so keep a condom handy. Excuse me, but there's an enormous difference between *difficult* and *impossible*. The notion that people can't restrain themselves is a totally bogus argument. I'm living proof that restraint *is* possible. Instead of urging readers to reach for a condom,

Landers should challenge them to reach for the inner strength to say NO!

Permit me one example. Let's say you're on a date. At one point things get a little out of hand and you proceed to the bedroom. Somewhere in the back of your brain an alarm sounds: STOP, DON'T DO IT! But you've ignored its warning and presently you are lying next to your date with your clothes off. Understandably, the hormones are spinning out of control, both bodies are sweating, and you feel like the freeway to ultimate sexual experiences lies wide before you.

Of course you feel there's no way you can apply the brakes. Now, let's imagine that immediately before consummating this act of improper passion your date said, "By the way, I'm HIV positive. We really ought to be using a condom." Without question—even this late in the act—you'd find a way to control yourself pronto!

> Instead of urging readers to reach for a condom, Landers should challenge them to reach for the inner strength to say NO!

Does it sound like I'm being too harsh? What about Masterton's blanket assertion that condoms are "the single most effective protection" against AIDS? And what of his belief that condoms will without question "prevent the spread of AIDS"? As we'll see in a moment, the proof is in the prophylactic.

Indecent Proposal

In 1994, the school board of education in Connecticut authorized the distribution of condoms to *fifth* graders. (One wonders if Landers was on their advisory board.) And why not pass out colorful condoms to kids as if they were candy canes. After all, back then Joycelyn Elders was in the driver's seat as Surgeon General—the highest medical authority in the land.

In her capacity, she spewed forth dim-witted advice like this classic: "We've taught [teenagers] what to do in the front seat. Now it's time to teach them what to do in the back seat."[20] She believed we ought to put our trust in rubbers and begin to preach the safe sex message as early as kindergarten! (Imagine Big Bird or Mister Rogers adding that topic to their repartee.)

Thankfully, Elders is out—and the evidence is in.

Concerning the reliability factor of prophylactic use, the real eye-opener was discovered by Dr. C. M. Roland, editor of *Rubber Chemistry & Technology*. He reports:

> The rubber comprising latex condoms has intrinsic voids about **5 microns** (0.0002 inches) in size. Since this is roughly 10 times smaller than sperm, the latter are effectively blocked in ideal circumstances ... Contrarily, the AIDS virus is only **0.1 microns** (4 millionths of an inch) in size. Since this is a factor of 50 smaller than the voids inherent in rubber, the virus can readily pass through the condom should it find a passage.[21]

Dr. Susan Weller is from the University of Texas. She wanted to discover condom efficacy in actual use. With this in mind, she conducted an analysis of data from eleven separate studies. Her findings are alarming. Dr. Weller discovered that condoms had an average failure rate of thirty-one percent in protecting against HIV. She writes:

> Since contraceptive research indicates condoms are about 90 percent effective in preventing pregnancy, many people, even physicians, assume condoms prevent HIV transmission with the same degree of effectiveness. However, HIV transmission studies do not show this to be true ... new data indicate some condoms, even latex ones, may leak HIV.[22]

Don't like the notion that condoms have a thirty-one percent failure rate when used to block HIV? Then what number would you prefer? How about the more conservative figure of twenty percent. Even with that widely agreed upon ratio, you'd have better odds of living if you played Russian roulette with a gun to your head (one in six chance) than to have sex with an infected partner (one in five chance).

There's one other dimension of this condom business I'd like to highlight before moving on. Debates over failure rates, pluses and minuses of their use, manufacturer defects, and the like miss the soul of the matter. Sex was created by God to strengthen the marital union. In addition to bringing pleasure to those who have made this lifelong pledge, he designed it to deepen the marriage vows.

Not surprisingly, many today want to take a shortcut across the fields of impatience and skim the cream from the top of the marital union. C. S. Lewis says it best:

> The monstrosity of sexual intercourse outside marriage is that those who indulge in it are trying to isolate one kind of union (the sexual) from all the other kinds of union which were intended to go along with it and make up the total union.
>
> The Christian attitude does not mean that there is anything wrong about sexual pleasure, any more than about the pleasure of eating. It means that you must not isolate that pleasure and try to get it by itself, any more than you ought to try to get the pleasures of taste without swallowing and digesting, by chewing things and spitting them out again.
>
> As a consequence, Christianity teaches that marriage is for life.[23]

My personal philosophy: If we singles have nothing to aspire to, we will always aspire to nothing. Tell me I can't control myself and I'll invariably sink into the sewer of unrestrained carnality. Inform me that, like the eagle I can soar above the gutter and fly freely in the great blue sky of self-discipline, and I'll catch the next updraft!

The Dating Dilemma

Back to our original question, "Would you marry someone who tested HIV positive?" I read with interest what the responders to my informal singles survey had to say. Here's a sample of their thinking. As you'll see, virtually without exception the answer was a resounding "NO WAY!" You can almost feel their passion leap off the page as they qualify their response:

Bob: "No. She would be a time bomb. I wouldn't want to live with the dread that I could lose her at anytime, not to mention the constant fear of contracting it myself."

Steph: "I may be suicidal at times, but that's not how I'd want to go!"

Stu: "No. We couldn't have children because they'd be born with it."

Rhoda: "Are you kidding? Sex is far too important to me."

Troy: "NO! *God* would have to personally tell me to."

Joey: "No. How could you enjoy sex worrying about contracting AIDS with every act?"

Jill: "No way. I didn't wait all of this time to marry someone who may die in a year."

Greg and Traci both leaned in the direction of saying yes but weren't altogether comfortable doing so. Greg writes, "If I found out early on, I would probably abandon ship. Maybe the 'savior complex' in me would keep me from exiting the relationship." Traci's perspective was similar.

Only one respondent offered an unqualified "yes." Liz explains, "God loves that person who is HIV positive and together we would pray for a cure." Many of those who said no also made it clear they would still love the infected person. At the same time, they believed such love didn't obligate them to marriage.

> You'd have better odds of living if you played Russian roulette with a gun to your head (1 in 6 chance) than to have sex with an infected partner (1 in 5 chance).

How would you answer the question?

Whether you know it or not, the way you respond profoundly impacts your approach to dating. Sooner than later this issue of sexual history must be discussed. But how and when?

Let's begin with the "how." Turn back with me to the responses to my survey on singles. Over all, I found the indirect and direct approaches used with about equal frequency. Only one person said he had no idea how to tackle this issue. If that's the case for you, maybe one of these ideas will give you a place to start.

Donna: I'd introduce the topic using a movie, newspaper article, or friend as a discussion starter. Or, if I saw a magazine cover story on the topic of sexual behavior, I'd bring it up the next time we're hanging out.

Stu: Sorry, but I'm afraid I'd be terribly blunt. I'd ask, 'So have you or haven't you engaged in premarital sex.' I wouldn't be judgmental, but I wouldn't dodge the issue just because it's a tough one. Raising a question like this over an informal meal seems to work best.

Tammy: I'd start with a more generic discussion of my values as they pertain to casual sex. If we happened to attend the same church, I might springboard off of a sermon on purity. Hopefully he'd follow my lead.

Dwayne: It seems to me that the guy should take the lead. I try to be vulnerable by introducing the subject first.

It's "lead by example" for me. My main objective is to address the issue when we have the time to get into it. Standing at her doorstep after a date isn't the right moment.

How far into the relationship should you tackle such a personal topic? Immediately? After several dates or months? Only if marriage was a strong possibility? In the minds of those in my survey, there doesn't appear to be a "right time." However, there was universal agreement that the discussion *must* take place.

Scott makes it a practice of asking before any kissing or physical displays of affection develop. Mary wonders, "Why put off the inevitable?" She'd cover the bases within the first two or three dates. Many thought marriage had to be on the table before ever talking about sexual history.

In my book that is too late—particularly for the single who would never marry someone with HIV. By waiting until marriage is on the map, you've allowed yourself to get emotionally, spiritually, and financially involved to such a deep degree that breaking things off will potentially create fierce hurt and bitterness. In my dating relationships, I've favored getting that information on the table as early as the new friendship can comfortably handle it.

Regardless of when you cross that bridge, the keys are to avoid a judgmental spirit. Assuming they did make a number of sexual mistakes along the way, if the Lord has forgiven them—and they've sought his forgiveness—then who am I not to? If they are clean in his sight, then they ought to be clean in our sight.

Those of us who are virgins should fight the temptation to operate from a position of pride. I know I've fought like a dog to remain chaste. It's so easy to cop an attitude, like "If I could, why couldn't you?" But God is not honored when we sport a "holier than thou" look.

A final dimension of the sexual history issue remains. If you learned that he or she had one or more sexual partners, how would you ask them to get tested for AIDS? Talk about a tough one. Matthew favored the direct approach. He said, "Read my lips: Get tested or I'm outta here!" For Karen, if he wasn't a virgin and didn't have an AIDS test, she wouldn't even consider a date!

Lynette would suggest to her boyfriend that they go down to the clinic and get tested together—that's one suggestion I highly concur with. Stephanie adds, "If they refuse to get tested—even with my willingness to be tested alongside of them—that would be a red flag. I'd wonder what they were trying to hide." Good point.

And Some People Eat Cars

There once was a man who was given this challenge: If he could *eat* a car in one year, he'd earn one million dollars. I forget where I read this fascinating story, but I remember the challenge was real—and he made the goal. How did he manage to accomplish such an unlikely feat?

Under a doctor's watchful eye, every day he would grind the various auto parts into a super fine powder. Then he'd sprinkle it on his food throughout the day. We're talking the roof, the engine—even the tires. (The gas, oil and other fluids were drained before the feast began.) Sounds real appetizing. As crazy of an objective as it was, he met his goal.

My point?

If you want something bad enough, you'll find a way to get it—no matter how far-fetched you are led to believe it is. Is sexual purity important to you? Do you desire to maximize your future happiness and sexual intimacy? Then throw the condom nonsense out the window. Forever cross it off of your list of options. Make a pledge to God that you will honor him with your sexuality. Work at becoming a godly lover.

Then devise a plan that will ensure success. Contemplate these important questions regarding sexual history and AIDS testing now while you still have time to think clearly.

This is not just an interesting academic brain tease.

It's a way of life.

CHAPTER 9

Hope for the Single Heart

Son, there are millions of singles who want
desperately to become married. But there are
also millions of restless married people who
wish they were single. The key is to learn how
to let the peace of God fill you no matter the
circumstance.

—*My dad*

Houses and wealth are inherited from parents,
but a prudent wife is from the LORD.

—*Proverbs 19:14*

Throughout this book you've heard me refer to a
singles survey. To provide you with a more specific
picture of the questions I asked hundreds of singles around the country, I've taken the liberty to reprint an
entire copy of the survey in appendix B. (I found it interesting to watch several dozen singles initially volunteer to
take part in the survey, only to back out after reviewing a
number of the more challenging questions.)

Take a moment to consider the last question I pitched to
those participating in the survey: What, if anything, is your
greatest fear at the prospect of remaining single for the rest
of your life?

Talk about a heavy question! And yet I believe it's an

appropriate one to conclude a book on sex and the single person. Why? With the amount of energy we exert fighting, controlling, and appropriately sharpening our sexual side, you'd think sex was of paramount importance to us. It would be reasonable to assume such a powerful force would rage until the end of our days.

Hard as it is to believe, no one directly mentioned missing out on sex as their primary anxiety over never marrying! In fact, remorse over foregoing sex didn't directly show up *anywhere* in their list of concerns. Talk about an amazing scoop . . . where's ABC's *20/20*?!

Listen to the *real* issues you and I care about as they pertain to a life of single service:

Pam: Not loneliness as much as a lack of being known and loved by one companion. The thought of not bonding in a special God-ordained way is scary to me!

Stu: Growing old—alone. No family. No children.

Betty: Not being able to be a mother. I love children so much it hurts inside.

Joey: The feelings of being left out, of missing out on the great joy of companionship.

Sandy: Not having anyone to come home to when I am older.

Jim: People may assume there's something wrong with me. Their skeptical rejection would be hard to take.

Vicki: Feeling as if people included me out of obligation or because they felt sorry for me.

Joan: Closing the door at the end of the day and feeling the echoing emptiness inside.

Barb: I worry that I won't have someone there to help me be strong when I'm weak. That I'll lack a teammate to serve the Lord with as we, together, reach out to those around us.

Cindi: Becoming lonely and bitter. Never having anyone to
share my hopes and dreams with . . . always feeling like
there was something I missed out on.

James used only two words to sum up his fear:
Being alone. Likewise, Roxanne chose a pair of words:
Dying alone. You see, when it comes down to what matters most in life, sex— although important and enjoyable—is a low priority. Granted, sex is involved to some
degree in each of their concerns. For instance, it's necessary
for children. But it was clearly not the thrill-seeking side of
sex that they longed to experience before death.

When the Beatles sang, "All you need is love," if they
were defining love primarily in terms of the act of sex, they
obviously missed the target by a long shot. Speaking of missing the mark, listen to Elton John. This British pop musician confessed,
"I'm a gay man
and have had a
lot of my friends
die . . . I slept with
half of America
and came out of
it HIV negative. I
was a lucky, lucky
person. I have a
second chance to
lead a decent
life."[1]

Is Elton John
gladdened sim-
ply because he
played the fool
and managed to
escape the conse-
quence of disease?

ZIGGY ©1995 ZIGGY & FRIENDS, INC. Dist. by
UNIVERSAL PRESS SYNDICATE. Reprinted with permission.

An endless string of one-night stands—is that what makes his soul sing? Ultimately, what gives life meaning? Great sex? Sex with strangers? Random lovers? Pornographic video fantasies? The "right" to engage in sex with a long-term boyfriend or girlfriend?

Singles who, like Elton John, participate in such a potpourri of sexual experimentation are just attempting to mask a deeper need—the God-shaped void inside their soul. They're afraid to face their fears. Sex is the narcotic to tranquilize the pain. (I might add, even Christian singles may be duped into thinking, "If only I could have sex, everything would be all right.")

St. Augustine lived such a life. His carefree consumption of sex and partying prior to his conversion was well documented. Looking back on his life he expressed the basic need of every human. In his *Confessions* Augustine writes, "Thou hast made us for Thyself, O Lord, and our hearts are restless until they rest in Thee."

Just look around you. At the office. In the bars. Or the cars parked on a dimly lit hillside. We're surrounded by a nation of people whose restlessness prompts them to reach daily for a cheap sexual sedative. In the process, they miss the Creator's perfect prescription to fill up their void—his Son Jesus.

Are you such a person? Then allow me a personal word.

I don't believe it's been an accident that you've eavesdropped on this book-long conversation about sex. Granted, you might think my perspective seems rather far out. That's understandable, especially if you've lived your life outside of a relationship with God. I realize the sexual choices you may have been making are closer to an Elton John than to a Bob DeMoss. You've spent your days believing the goal of sex was to reach orgasmic joy. Different partners? You've accepted the notion that the more the merrier—as long as you played "safe."

Now you read a book written by the oldest virgin you've ever come in contact with. You hear that he's happy and enjoys life to the fullest. You see that sex for most singles is low on their priority of lifelong aspirations. You've discovered that a richer sexual intimacy exists, and that there are a multitude of nonsexual ways to cultivate satisfying personal intimacy.

> We're surrounded by a nation of people whose restlessness prompts them to reach daily for a cheap sexual sedative.

But such a goal seems outside of your grasp. Why?

For years you've been playing the part of a runaway child who refuses to come home. Like the Prodigal Son, you keep throwing your body—and caution—into the wind. You're under the illusion that if you stop the conquest game playing, your very identity will evaporate. You've grown accustomed to this way of living, and fear holds on to your feet like a ball and chain preventing you from making a change.

Yet tonight the streets have lost their appeal. Playing in the sexual highway, as we saw in the previous chapter, is sure to get you run over. Perhaps at long last you desire to make a change. You hunger for peace inside and you can tell from experience that sex isn't filling the void.

Do you know how to break the chain of fear that binds you?

Perfect Love Casts Out All Fear

I'm sure glad God didn't create the world and then take an eternal vacation from his creation. He watched with the eyes of a loving father as humankind fell from grace. When Adam and Eve opened the door to sin, God knew it would wreak havoc on the rest of history. Just as a knife can destroy a Picasso in an instant, sin sliced through his incredible design for sexual intimacy in a second.

In his wisdom, the Lord knew we'd use our feeble resources to piece things back together—or at least masquerade as if there was no problem. Rather than allow humankind to wallow in hopeless fear and pain, he provided a solution. Matt, the last respondent to my survey, put it this way:

> God be praised for his promise, "perfect love drives out fear" (1 John 4:18). That's why intimacy with God—not sex—is the best antidote for discontentment as a single, even when staring in the face of life-long singleness!

Intimacy with God.

It sounds so simple, but how does a rebel make his peace with God? The great news of the Bible is that we can be put right with the Creator of the universe if we—by faith—will believe in Jesus (Acts 16:31). It was Jesus who paid the price for all of our sins—including our sexual excesses—so that we might be welcomed with open arms into the family of God. One of the most familiar verses of the Bible explains:

> For God so loved the world that he gave his one and only Son, that whoever *believes* in him shall not perish but have eternal life. For God did not send his Son into the world to condemn the world, but to save the world through him. (John 3:16–17, emphasis added)

Do you desire to find the inner peace that sex isn't capable of supplying? Do you want the *quality* of your relationships with men and women to take a quantum leap forward? Would you like to feel God's peace gently nurturing your malnourished soul? Then invite Jesus into your heart.

I'd like to point you to the book *Power for Living*. This wonderful resource explains in simple terms how to enter into a right relationship with God. I encourage you to write and request a complimentary copy: *Power for Living*, Box 1000, South Holland, IL 60473. Then, as you get intimate with God, you'll find yourself energized in ways no sexual high could ever produce.

Guaranteed.

For the Love of God

A word to the Christian single. Maybe you haven't been trespassing in the fields of stolen passion. Unlike Elton John, Madonna, Prince, Janet Jackson, or any other pop star who celebrates illicit sex, you've managed to abstain. Oh, you've given it some thought—and the emotional cycle we discussed in chapter 5 routinely pushes you closer to the edge. But for now you've stayed on track.

Let me assure you, there *will* come a time when your resolve will be tested under maximum pressure.

In those moments, you'll wonder if God is really trustworthy. Is his plan for you actually in your best interests? He's made you wait ... and wait ... and, well, years have passed and you're still waiting. Although such thoughts will

> **As you get intimate with God, you'll find yourself energized in ways no sexual high could ever produce.**

present themselves, don't give them the time of day. Just as Joseph refused to play footsie with Potiphar's wife, refuse to entertain those eternally destructive thoughts. He *can* be trusted.

Lying in bed late at night, one of my favorite things to do is read the writings of Chuck Swindoll. Talk about a master writer! In the following passage he poignantly confronts this matter of dependence on God. And I love the way Swindoll reminds us that God is very much in control—even over our desire for a spouse and sexual intimacy. Watch out, my man Chuck doesn't mince any words:

> Honestly now, do you think God's control over us is total ... or partial? ... Accept it or not, God's calling the

shots. He's running the show. Either He's in *full* control or He's off His throne. It's as foolish to say He's "almost sovereign" as it would be to say I'm "almost married" or Kennedy was "almost president" or the surgeon's gloves are "almost sterile."

If you're trying to grasp all the ramifications of this great truth . . . don't. You can't anyway. Feverishly toiling to unravel all the knots can turn you into a fanatical freak . . . it will push you to the edge of your mental capacity . . . it will result in endless hours of theological hairsplitting. The finite can never plumb the depths of the infinite . . . so don't waste your time trying.

> **Far too many spend their days driving down the highway of life constantly looking in the rearview mirror fearful their past will catch up with them.**

It was a glorious day when I was liberated from the concentration camp of fear . . . the fear of saying, "I don't understand the reasons why, but I accept God's hand in what has happened." One of the marks of spiritual maturity is the quiet confidence that God is in control . . . without the need to understand why He does what He does.[2]

God's plan will be for our *best*. Do you believe it? Will you trust him? Then don't ignore his directions as outlined in the Scriptures. When he says "save sex for marriage," *listen* to him. Since we're commanded to "flee sexual immorality," *just do it*—don't ask questions. Trust that God knew what he was doing when he provided these laws.

In her song "Streets of Innocence," singer Margaret Becker celebrated the joys of such obedience. She described it as sleeping "on the bed of no regrets." Far too many spend their days driving down the highway of life constantly looking in the rearview mirror, fearful their past will catch up with them. Not Becker. She looks to the future with a clear conscience because of her decision to obey God's Word.

Those who ignore his rules can count on a lifetime of trouble and regrets. And when it comes to sex in this era, such disregard might get you killed. One personal example of my failure to follow the rules—and the resulting consequences—might help you understand why I now take such a strong stance on obedience.

Why the Spiritual Wear Goggles

Recently I was playing racquetball with a friend. Fans of this fast-paced sport know that protective eye wear is *highly* recommended. Still, I have played for many years without goggles—in spite of the advisories.

On that fateful evening, I remember catching a glimpse of the warning sign strategically placed on the court door. *Yeah, yeah, I've seen it before*, I thought as I characteristically ignored its advice. Bad idea. After serving the game's opening point, I glanced back to see where the ball had landed. Within seconds, I received a direct hit to my right eye. Time stood still.

When I arrived at the emergency ward, the doctor asked me what I could see out of my injured eye. I was in such pain that I couldn't tell if my eye was even open. He confirmed that it was. But I couldn't see a thing.

That evening, as I rested in the hospital, many thoughts raced through my mind. It's true that we don't really appreciate something until it's gone. Naturally, I reflected on the gift of sight. Not knowing if I'd ever see out of that eye again, I found myself taking inventory. A number of Bible passages came to mind—those describing the eye as the lamp of the soul.

For example, Matthew 6:22–23 says, "The eye is the lamp of the body. If your eyes are good, your whole body will be full of light. But if your eyes are bad, your whole body will be full of darkness. If then the light within you is darkness, how great is that darkness." These verses have taken on new meaning to me. (I'm thankful to report that most of my vision has returned—and I've already purchased two sets of goggles, one for me and one for my *partner*!)

During my recovery period, I thought it might be interesting to conduct a Bible word search. I decided to count the number of times Scripture speaks of our eyes, or uses imagery related to vision. My hunch was that God places a premium on the gift of sight.

I searched for words like "see," "look," "blind," "sight," and so on. Did you know there are 3,059 uses of such words? For the sake of comparison, I tallied biblical references using other anatomical imagery. Those relating to the "heart" numbered 570. Mentions of our "head" and related words totaled 869. Our "hands," 1,733 times. "Feet" numbered 1,069. Finally, I looked to the gift of our ears with 1,071 references to them.

Reviewing my list, it appeared the "eyes" have it. (Sorry.)

So what's the lesson in all of this? Simply that you and I have been given something very special—the gift of sight. So precious and critical are our eyes, the Bible refers to them more often than any other part of our body. Matthew 6:22–23 takes it one step further when it makes it clear we must guard what we set in front of our eyes.

You see, this gift is subject to many temptations—temptations to engage in evil imagery, like sexually explicit videotapes, R-rated movies, saucy cable programs, swimsuit issues, and in the not too distant future the vile realm of "virtual reality" sex. In the midst of this depraved environment God warns us to "set no worthless thing" before our eyes (Ps. 101:3 NAS). Why? Because he desires to protect us from the consequences.

To fill our mind with an endless stream of sexual images

is to invite trouble. To ignore his rules pertaining to sexual choices before marriage is to sever intimacy with Jesus. That's why every day we need to put on our "spiritual eye-goggles" to protect our mind and to prevent spiritual blindness.

I, to borrow a phrase, "won't leave home without them."

Body Language

Having considered our mind, now a word about our bodies.

So far I've said precious little about the physical fitness and relative health of those who filled out the singles survey. Although I did not have an opportunity to meet each of the participants, I did view many via a photograph. Some were striking in dress and physique while others didn't pay much attention to their appearance. If I were to offer an estimate, I'd have to say upwards of *forty percent* fell into the latter category—they simply looked unkempt and unhealthy.

In addition, as a speaker who travels widely, I've met many singles in person to discuss various aspects of this book. Time after time I'd conclude a meeting and think to myself, "That guy needs to be introduced to a razor," or "She'd do herself a favor to occasionally gargle with Listerine." I don't want to appear mean, but there is nothing spiritual about breath that precedes our presence!

If this informal observation has any merit, I'm afraid that the older you and I get, the less likely we are to spend time on physical conditioning and personal hygiene. Let's face it. Unless we singles live with a roommate who has a strong sense of propriety, we unfortunately don't have a spouse to remind us to trim nose and ear hair, to brush the dandruff off, to suggest a new mouthwash, or to challenge us to spend thirty minutes sweating on the exercise bike.

Nor do we have someone that will be honest and tell us when it's time to discard the bell-bottom jeans and other outdated clothing. In other words, while we prepare our

There is nothing spiritual about breath that precedes our presence.

mind, our spirit, and our hearts to be a godly lover (which has been the obvious emphasis of this book), we would be wise to invest in our health and personal presentation as well.

Actually, I'm a little surprised to hear myself touching on this topic. You see, although I am conscious of most hygiene issues, I seriously doubt that anyone would ever confuse me with a hyper-health-conscious-carrot-juice-drinking-physical-perfectionist. But I've recently come to the conclusion that if I desire to sweep a lady off of her feet, it's a package deal: my spirit and my body must be well maintained.

I fear that Christian singles may tend to neglect caring for their bodies (and their wardrobes) as a reaction against a society which seems obsessed with such matters. Both extremes should be avoided. Frankly, after hitting thirty I didn't work as hard to wrestle with my scale. It wasn't long before an extra thirty pounds took residence on my frame. The added weight complicated my wardrobe which directly and negatively affected the way I felt about myself.

Several weeks ago I made a decision to get serious about my personal conditioning. It wasn't easy but I agreed to get up every morning at 4:30 in order to be at the gym by 5:00 A.M. for a two-hour workout. At first, all the cells in my body informed me that they hated me! After five weeks of this grueling Monday through Friday routine, my body actually thanked me. Back and stomach muscles were stronger, the waistline trimmer. The spring started to return to my step!

Please understand that I'm trying to strike a balance here. Yes, our spiritual development and emotional maturity is foundational. At the same time, keeping our body clean and healthy should be part of our agenda—both now and after the wedding bells sound. (I'm told the added attention to physical conditioning will also go a long way toward maximizing the wonderful expression of sex in marriage.)

Do you need to spend a little less time behind a desk and more time on a treadmill? Are you feeling the need to drop a few extra pounds and tone the muscles you have? Why not take six months to redirect some of your energy toward improving your personal presentation. Find a workout partner to keep you accountable. Chart your progress on the refrigerator. Consider sprucing up your wardrobe with a few new items.

Between this and the spiritual preparation we've discussed in the previous chapters, I can't think of a better way to make the most of these moments. So go for it and seize the time while you still can!

The Price Is Right

Have you ever been in a photographic darkroom? They don't call it "dark" for nothing. It's pitch black. In this light-starved environment, the professional photographer exposes a piece of photo paper to a negative image and dunks it in a tray of developer. There, in total darkness, that negative is subjected to acidic conditions for a designated period of time.

If the paper were removed from the tray too quickly, it would be an underdeveloped, worthless print. But given just the right amount of processing time, the photo that emerges will be simply picture perfect.

In some ways, gaining the proper perspective on sex and intimacy is like the process necessary to develop a photograph. At times, you and I may feel like we're completely in the dark. We don't understand why God has us in a holding pattern. Complicating our feelings is the acid of peer pressure, media stimuli, and hormonal surges which splash against our resolve. We're tempted to jump out of the Master's tray before he's through preparing us.

If we rush the process, we'll miss the beautiful picture of

what might have been. I'm thankful that years ago my youth pastor challenged us not to rush the procedure.

Back in high school I once heard the expression, "She's not the kind of girl you'd bring home to your mother." The subject was dating—or should I say whom *not* to date. We were having one of *those* youth group meetings where the youth pastor was painting a picture of a godly spouse. As you might guess, his text was Proverbs 31:10–31.

The passage begins, "An excellent wife, who can find? For her worth is far above jewels" (NAS). The extraordinary attributes of a godly woman are then described. Sitting on the floor with my legs crossed, I remember making a silent commitment to seek such a woman. But I took it a step further. I pledged to work at becoming a godly lover as well. Why? If and when the Lord brings us together, I want to serve this priceless gem with excellence.

If we rush the process, we'll miss the beautiful picture of what might have been.

Would you like to make a similar commitment today? You can. Do you have the guts to stay in the darkroom withstanding the corrosive pressures until the Master photographer says it's time to show the world your stuff? Great. Then bathe in the four principles of this book. By way of review they are:

- Marriage and sex should *not* be our objective—rather, becoming a godly lover is the goal.

- Cultivate the fine art of intimacy. Leave the immature (and unfulfilling) conquest game-playing to the dead-end club scene.

- Recognize that emotions are like a drunk driver. Unless we steer it correctly, our emotional cycle will invariably attempt to push our sex drive off of the moral high road.

- Learn how to be an awesome, godly lover from those who are doing it right.

Even at thirty-seven, I enthusiastically wait upon the Lord to see what develops!

APPENDIX A

Pro-Active Abstinence

Besides applying the principles of this book, you and I have plenty of other constructive applications of our time and energy. Like what? Mission one: try confronting the out-of-control culture we live in. Write letters. Boycott trashy programs. Challenge the broadcasters who inflict socially harmful material on the populace to give an account for such irresponsible activity.

The battle is raging in communities all across this great nation. Is Howard Stern polluting your air waves with talk of lesbian sex? Help him find another job. Put pressure on the local station that carries him. Has your school board of education authorized the distribution of condoms to fifth graders? Help them understand why such a course of action fails.

But be realistic. As you apply the higher standard of sexual intimacy that we've covered in these pages, don't expect the media elite to readily embrace your efforts. Take, for example, what happened to the Christian musician Michael Sweet.

As I wrote these pages, I noticed Sweet's skirmish with Music Television. This former lead singer of Stryper wanted to voice an opposing point of view to MTV's safe sex message. The video for his song, "Ain't No Safe Way" was a compelling production that caught MTV with its corporate pants down. It struck such a sour note with the management of MTV that these advocates of "free speech" refused to air his video.

When Sweet's record company submitted "Ain't No Safe Way," MTV refused to air it. Why? Two reasons. First, they said it didn't meet their minimum standards of video production quality. Second, they maintained that Sweet was an unknown artist. Of course! What else are they going to say.

Sweet is one of the hottest artists in Christian music today. His well-crafted video competes with the best of MTV's lineup. As a member of Stryper, he had two number-one videos on MTV several years prior.

MTV's explanations ring hollow. It seems to me they simply couldn't bear the thought of Sweet's vote for abstinence reining in their twenty-four-hour masturbatory fantasy. Interesting. It looks like MTV believes in freedom of speech just as long as you don't disagree with their philosophical position.

A few lines from his song reveal why MTV probably balked:

You say it can't happen, won't happen to you . . .
And you think that you're protected and invincible, too.
If you play with fire, then you're gonna get burned.
Better change your desire, or the hard way you will
    learn.
Tell me man, how does it measure?
To risk it all for a little pleasure?
Ain't no safe way anymore.
You got people with one, two, three, and four.
Abstinence rules, playin' is for fools,
The one who abstains is the one who's cool
There's no safe way.[1]

As he sang, statistics of condom failure rates, teen pregnancy, annual abortion figures, and current STD data flashed on the screen behind him! No wonder MTV refused.

My point is that whether you have the talent to write a song, produce a video, or simply write a letter or make a phone call, your efforts may fall upon deaf ears. But don't let that stop you from trying! We must work to stem the tide of this moral free fall. America needs champions for chastity now more than ever.

Will you be one?

APPENDIX B

The Singles Survey

In preparation for this book, I invited a cross-section of single adults to provide their perspective on this intensely personal subject. Although I've had over two decades of personal experience being single, I wanted to "get inside" the heads of others who walk the same miles but who can share another perspective. The youngest single to complete the survey was 21, while the oldest was 42. Virtually all indicated they were certain of a conversion to Christ experience.

As you review the original survey reprinted herein, you'll notice a number of questions are rather intimate. Those who volunteered to respond were encouraged to skip those items they did not feel comfortable answering, and were assured that names, cities, and other potentially identifying elements would be changed to protect their privacy.

You might enjoy considering how you'd respond to the survey. In fact, it could be the perfect way to tackle some of the more difficult questions you and a serious dating partner should be discussing. Feel free to make copies as needed for your personal use. If you are working with a small group setting, kindly indicate this book as the original source for the document.

And, have fun getting at these hard issues!

Personal Data

Name _____ Age ____
Address _____ Female/Male ____
City/State _____
Christian (yes/no/unsure) _____

Phone (_____) _____
Church affiliation _____

1. Status (check one)

   _____ Single, never married.
   _____ Single, divorced.
   (Number of years since the divorce was finalized: _____)
   _____ Single, widowed.
   (Number of years since your spouse's death: _____)

2. If previously married, do you have children? Yes, no.

   How many? _____

3. Do you believe you have the "gift" of singleness, or are
   you actively interested in finding a marriage partner?

Sexual History

1. If never married, are you still a virgin? (Y/N) _____

   If widowed or divorced, were you a virgin at the time of
   your marriage? (Y/N) _____

2. If you are single, never married and not a virgin, how
   many different sexual partners have you had? _____

3. Have you ever been tested for HIV/AIDS? (Y/N) _____

4. Has anyone you've dated ever requested that you be
   tested for AIDS? If so, do you recall how they asked you
   to get the test?
   How did their request make you feel? Threatened?
   Offended? Put off? Explain.

5. If you are not a virgin (for whatever reason, including
   through a marriage experience), has your past sexual

involvement complicated your ability to abstain now? Why?

6. Regardless of your sexual history, do you believe premarital sex is wrong? Furthermore, describe whether you find it easy, somewhat difficult, very difficult, or impossible to abstain while waiting for marriage.

7. What ideas or strategies can you suggest to keep your God-given hormones in check?

8. If you are still a virgin, how do you think society (defined as peers, work associates, the media, and Hollywood) views you?

9. Can you provide any passages of Scripture that have been helpful to you as you've sought to be sexually pure in our morally bankrupt society?

10. What is your opinion of the "everyone is doing it, so just use a condom" message that teenagers are being taught at school today?

11. Besides "because God says so," can you provide several reasons and benefits for remaining a virgin until marriage?

Emotional Responses

1. Assuming marriage is a personal goal for you, explain why you desire to be married.

2. How do you feel when married friends suggest, "Perhaps God has kept you single in order that you can do more kingdom work"?

3. Have you read any books on the subject of singleness? If so, list the names of them.

   Which ones did you find especially helpful? Why?

4. List several advantages of being single.

5. List several aspects of singleness that cause you the most grief or pain.

6. Typically speaking, what is your emotional state on February 14?

7. By what age did you originally believe you'd be married? And, what (if anything) happened to your emotions when several years slipped past this date and you were still single?

8. Have you ever been mad or disappointed with God because of your singleness? Describe those feelings, what led to them, and how you've resolved your anger (if you've resolved it).

9. Have you ever been engaged? (Y/N) ____ If more than once, how many times? ____

10. Why did the engagement end?

11. Do you experience pressure from family or friends to get married? Provide several ways that you have experienced this pressure and how you handle it.

12. Is having children important to you? (Y/N) ____

13. For women responders: Does the prospect of growing too old to bear children cause you to panic? How do you come to terms with the fact that you might not get married in time?

    For men responders: Does the childbearing ability of a prospective date play a factor in your decision to pursue a particular woman? And, do you find yourself feeling pressure to make a move toward marriage because she is sensitive to the biological time line?

14. How are you tempted to behave when your singleness gets weary? (Check those which apply):

    ____ I'll visit a dance club or bar in order to meet someone new.

_____ I use alcohol to numb the emptiness.

_____ I turn to pornography.

_____ I'll re-ignite a relationship with a former boyfriend/girlfriend even when I know it's unhealthy to do such.

_____ I go on a binge spree.

_____ Other outlet:

Take a minute to develop the process of dealing with the temptations you've indicated.

15. Do you have a close friend who can help you remain accountable? If so, describe the role he or she plays in your life and how they've helped you.

Dating Dynamics

1. Are you now, or have you ever regularly participated in a singles ministry at church? If so, briefly describe your involvement, including how long you've been involved, the group size, the value or challenge you experience by attending, and so on.

   If you have not attended a singles outreach, explain the reasons that keep you from doing so. Be honest.

2. Are you currently seriously dating anyone? (Y/N) _____ For how many months? _____

3. How many dates have you been on during the last year?

   _____ None

   _____ Less than 5

   _____ 6 to 12

   _____ Several dozen

   _____ Too many to count

   _____ What's a date?

4. Would you marry someone who you knew tested HIV positive? Why, or why not?

5. Picture this. You've met someone you really like. You believe there's mutual interest of something serious developing. Given the backdrop of AIDS and other life-threatening sexually transmitted diseases, *how* would you approach the subject of his/her past sexual history?

   At *what point* in the relationship would you cross this bridge? Immediately? After several dates or months? Only if marriage was a strong possibility? Never? Why?

   Further, if you learned that he/she had one or more sexual partners, *would* you ask for them to get tested for AIDS? Secondly, *how* would you ask them to get tested?

6. Describe some of your favorite (most memorable) dating experiences. What made them so?

7. Have you ever had a "date from hell"? If so, what made it such a bad experience?

8. Have you ever turned an invitation to go on a date down? If yes, why?

9. Have you ever found yourself compromising your values in order to enter or hang on to a relationship that you knew in your heart was unhealthy? Why?

10. During a "dry spell" (where you've gone quite a while without dating anyone) chances are that you've experienced a degree of restlessness and frustration. Can you identify several sources that may have amplified your feelings of unhappiness as a single? (Consider the influence of romance novels, R-rated films, weddings, newborn babies, or television shows in your answer.)

11. Are you aware of any areas in your life (be it spiritual, physical, emotional, financial, etc.) that you really need to work on which might be keeping you from growing

as a single adult with strong possibilities for marriage? Explain.

12. What is the purpose of dating in your book? Do you have an agenda when you go on a date?

13. Generally speaking, how quickly into a new relationship do you find yourself deciding whether or not you have interest to develop it into something special? Provide a few of the criteria that you use to arrive at your decision.

14. Have you ever dated a Christian who applied pressure to have sexual intercourse? How did you respond? How did their pressure make you feel?

15. On the whole, do you think you have a healthy view of dating?

Summary Issues

1. What is the primary lesson(s) about your lot in life as a single adult that you've learned?

2. What advice/insight would you like to pass on to other singles if you could say anything to them?

3. Are there any Scripture references that have helped to keep your eyes fixed on Jesus? Explain why they've been meaningful to you.

4. Are there any questions/issues that you feel a book on singleness ought to address?

5. What, if anything, is your greatest fear at the prospect of remaining single for life?

Notes

Acknowledgments

1. Bruce Felton, *One of a Kind* (New York: Quill William Morrow, 1992), 118.

Introduction

1. Dr. Laurence J. Peter, *Peter's Quotations* (New York: Quill, 1977), 441.

2. Robert G. DeMoss, Jr., *Learn to Discern* (Grand Rapids: Zondervan, 1992), *ix*.

Chapter One: Virgin Territory

1. Christopher Andersen, *Madonna Unauthorized*, epilogue (1991).

2. "Fatherhood? Not Yet," *Focus on the Family*, June 1993.

3. Robert Andrews, *The Columbia Dictionary of Quotations* (New York: Columbia University Press, 1993), 959.

4. "Fatherhood? Not Yet," *Focus on the Family*, June 1993.

5. Dr. Archibald D. Hart, *The Sexual Man* (Dallas: Word Publishing, 1994), 27.

6. "Fatherhood? Not Yet," *Focus on the Family*, June 1993.

Chapter Two: Sex and Intimacy: Listening to Those Who Are Married

1. Roseanne Barr discussing her divorce from Tom Arnold on the *Late Show with David Letterman* (September 7, 1994).

Chapter Three: The Fine Art of Intimacy

1. Charles R. Swindoll, *Strike the Original Match* (Grand Rapids: Zondervan, 1980), 44.

2. Dr. Gabrielle Brown, *The New Celibacy: A Journey to Love, Intimacy, and Good Health in a New Age* (New York: McGraw-Hill, 1989), 71.

3. Jennifer Allen, "Hanging with the Spur Posse," *Rolling Stone*, July 8–12, 1993.

4. "Where 'Boys Will Be Boys,' and Adults Are Bewildered," *The New York Times*, March 29, 1993.

5. Jennifer Allen, "Hanging with the Spur Posse," *Rolling Stone*, July 8–12, 1993.

6. Ibid.
7. Ibid.

Chapter Four: Single, Again

1. Robert Andrews, *The Columbia Dictionary of Quotations* (New York: Columbia University Press, 1993), 831.

2. Dr. Bobbie Reed, *Life After Divorce* (St. Louis: Concordia Publishing House, 1993), 165.

3. Anthony Robbins, *Awaken the Giant Within* (New York: Summit Books, 1991), 25.

Chapter Five: The Single Cycle

1. Jerry B. Jenkins, *Loving Your Marriage Enough to Protect It* (Chicago: Moody, 1989), 44.

2. "Desperate Women Answer Ad for Affair," *Gazette Telegraph*, August 13, 1993, F4.

3. C. H. Spurgeon, *Evening by Evening* (Springdale, Pa.: Whitaker, 1984), 69.

Chapter Six: How to Handle Those Hormones

1. Dr. Archibald D. Hart, *The Sexual Man* (Dallas: Word Publishing, 1994), 190.

2. Dr. James Dobson, *Romantic Love* (Ventura, Calif.: Regal Books, 1989), 39.

3. Dr. Gabrielle Brown, *The New Celibacy* (New York: McGraw-Hill, 1989), 39.

4. "The Virginity Comeback," *Single Adult Ministries* 108 (1995), 1.

5. Ibid., 3.

6. Bill and Pam Farrel, Jim and Sally Conway, *Pure Pleasure* (Downers Grove, Ill.: InterVarsity Press, 1994), 80.

7. Marjorie Holms, *I've Got to Talk to Somebody, God* (New York: Doubleday, 1969), 48–49.

Chapter Seven: Becoming a Great Lover

1. Gary Smalley with John Trent, *Love Is a Decision* (Dallas: Word Publishing, 1989), 40.

2. Bill Watterson, *Calvin and Hobbes* (New York: The Trumpet Club, 1987), 46.

3. Gregory J. P. Godek, *1001 Ways to be Romantic* (Weymouth, Mass.: Casablanca Press, 1991), 39.

Chapter Eight: Before You Kiss, Read This

1. Edited by John Daintith and Amanda Isaacs, *Medical Quotes: A Thematic Dictionary* (New York: Facts on File, 1989), 182.

2. Cal Thomas, *The Things That Matter Most* (New York: Harper-Collins, 1994), 84.

3. Dr. Paul C. Reisser, *Sex and Singles, Reasons to Wait* (Colorado Springs, Colo.: Focus on the Family, 1993), 6.

4. Dr. Joe McIlhaney, Jr., *Sexuality and Sexually Transmitted Diseases* (Grand Rapids: Baker, 1990), 19.

5. Ibid., 142.

6. Reisser, *Sex and Singles*, 5.

7. Centers for Disease Control, Division of STD/HIV Prevention, *1991 Annual Report* (Centers for Disease Control, 1992), 3.

8. Reisser, *Sex and Singles*, 7.

9. McIlhaney, *Sexuality and Sexually Transmitted Diseases*, 14.

10. Dr. James C. Dobson, *Love for a Lifetime* (Sisters, Ore.: Questar Publishers, 1993), 28.

11. U.S. Department of Health and Human Services, Public Health Service, Centers for Disease Control, 1991 Division of STD/HIV Prevention *Annual Report*, 13.

12. McIlhaney, *Sexuality and Sexually Transmitted Diseases*, 14.

13. Reisser, *Sex and Singles*, 6.

14. Felicity Barringer, "Viral Sexual Diseases are Found in One in Five in the U.S.," *The New York Times*, April 1, 1993, A–1.

15. Graham Masterton, *Single, Wild, Sexy . . . and Safe* (New York: Signet, 1994), 13.

16. Ibid., 24.

17. Ibid., 248.

18. Ibid., 248.

19. Ibid., 249.

20. Suzanne Fields, "Listening to Elders and Saying No," *The Washington Times*, July 15, 1993.

21. C. M. Roland, letter to the editor, *The Washington Times*, April 22, 1992, G–2.

22. Susan C. Weller, "A Meta-Analysis of Condom Effectiveness in Reducing Sexually Transmitted HIV," *Social Science & Medicine* 36 (June 1993), 1635–44.

23. Wayne Martindale and Jerry Root, *The Quotable Lewis* (Wheaton, Ill.: Tyndale House, 1989), 419.

Chapter Nine: Hope for the Single Heart

1. "Lucky in Life," *Entertainment Weekly*, February 10, 1995, 8.

2. Charles R. Swindoll, *Growing Strong in the Seasons of Life* (Portland, Ore.: Multnomah Press, 1983), 268–69.

Appendix A: Pro-Active Abstinence

1. "Ain't No Safe Way" by Michael Sweet © 1994 Benson Music Group, Inc. All rights reserved. Used by permission.